Home

Home

THE BEST OF The New York Times HOME SECTION

THE WAY WE LIVE NOW

Edited by Noel Millea of *The New York Times*

RIZZOLI
NEW YORK

New York · Paris · London · Milan

First published in the United States of America in 2017
by Rizzoli International Publications, Inc.
300 Park Avenue South
New York, NY 10010
www.rizzoliusa.com

2017 2018 2019 2020 / 10 9 8 7 6 5 4 3 2 1

Distributed in the U.S. trade by Random House, New York

Printed in China
Design by Kenneth McFarlin
Photo editing by Phaedra Brown

ISBN-13: 978-0-8478-5995-5
Library of Congress Control Number: 2017941773

CONTENTS

INTRODUCTION

Making a place that feels like home isn't easy, even for the lucky few who can spend whatever it takes. What comforts you, what inspires you, what you aspire to — all of this, and more, goes into designing a space that represents, on a small scale, the world you want to live in.

Not that most of us think that way. We focus on (or obsess about) finding the right sofa, or a good reading light, or an affordable rug, or maybe finally remodeling the kitchen.

Some people, though, take it much further, creating environments that are at once so strikingly personal and so exquisitely turned out that the rest of us can only marvel. For several years, as the editor of *The New York Times's* Home section, I was in the enviable position of getting paid to seek out and publish the stories of homes like these, a number of which are collected in this book.

What the people behind these homes share isn't a common design sensibility or approach to domestic life, but the commitment to a particular vision. At a time when much of the world seems to be growing ever more homogenous, here is proof that individuality is alive and flourishing.

How else to account for this wildly varied array of extraordinary spaces? The impeccably minimalist one-room cabin in upstate New York, for example, where a couple chose to raise two young children to teach them the value of living with less, or the ornate St. Petersburg apartment decked out in early Stalinist style, the owner's unconventional way of celebrating the beauty of the Soviet past while also acknowledging its ugliness. Or the tiny gingerbread house in the woods, built by hand on a minuscule budget, as solace for being homeless as a teen. Or the Nantucket house furnished almost entirely with eBay finds to create the illusion of a family legacy. Or the West Village apartment that transports you to the 1930s but was a step into the future for its occupant, whose previous place replicated the 19th century.

It's hard to read stories like these without fantasizing about alternate lives you yourself might lead, with a little imagination and a singular vision of your own. That's how I often felt, at least. The fixer-upper chateau in the Loire Valley was the one that really got to me. What if that impossible dream turned out to be not so impossible after all?

Sadly, the Home section is no more — it fell victim to a paper-wide restructuring — but with this book, these homes and their stories live on. And with them, perhaps, a few of those impossible dreams.

IT'S MOURNING IN AMERICA

BY PENELOPE GREEN • PHOTOGRAPHS BY BRUCE BUCK

Growing up in Uniontown, Pa., the Hurley twins, Tracy and Tonya, spent most weekends attending funerals with their grandmother. "In our hometown, Sundays were either for funerals or a Steelers game," said Tracy, who is now Tracy Martin. "And our grandmother was a funeral fly."

Funerals were also the family business. Their great-uncle Vito ran a funeral parlor, and he and his wife and five daughters lived upstairs. "It was just like working in a deli," Ms. Martin said. "Gorgeous cousin Denise" was the mortician, and when the twins' father, a boxer and

irregular presence in their lives, died of a heart attack when he was 42 and they were 19 and attending college (the first members of their family to do so), Denise laid him out. "He looks like hell," Ms. Martin recalled her saying. "I'll see what I can do."

One April afternoon, Ms. Martin, the chief executive of the Morbid Anatomy Museum, in Gowanus, Brooklyn — think peculiar Victorian taxidermy, illustrations of medical pathologies and preserved insects, among other cultish curiosities — and Ms. Hurley, the author of best-selling young-adult novels starring dead heroines (specifically teenage martyrs and ghosts), sat side by side at Ms. Martin's dining room table and tried to explain their own family business, their lifelong obsession with death and how Ms. Martin came to be the

overseer of a cultural institution devoted to the dead and the ghastly.

"We find joy in the macabre," Ms. Martin began. "It's fertile."

The setting was perfect: a late-19th-century Brooklyn brownstone that had been given a kind of Morbid Anatomy makeover by Robin Standefer and Stephen Alesch, the former movie-set designers now known for their highbrow, Steampunk-ish domestic and hotel interiors. There were black-and-yellow poppies in a vase and, on the wall, a stupendous Victorian mourning wreath. A black leather Dunbar sofa wore a hulking buffalo skin.

Ms. Martin and Ms. Hurley wore similar (though not identical) black tunics, black tights and boots. As Ms. Hurley said, "We will wear black until they invent a

The Park Slope home has been reworked to look as if it was furnished early in the last century. The 19th-century leather stools in the living room are Spanish; they sit on a vintage Berber rug.

8

darker color."

Every few minutes, a burst of electronic music wafted up from the basement. Ms. Martin is married to Vince Clarke, the English synth-pop star who is a founding member of Depeche Mode and half of the band Erasure. Mr. Clarke was on deadline for a new Erasure album and had been holed up for days in his basement studio with an arsenal of analog synthesizers.

The family business is music, films, books and now a museum (Ms. Hurley is on the board), much of it with a dark side. Ms. Hurley is married to Michael Pagnotta, a music and brand manager whose company, Reach, used to employ both sisters and who has handled not only Erasure, Depeche Mode, Morrissey, George Michael, Prince and the Cure, but also the Olsen twins. "We were the twins behind the twins," Ms. Martin said.

The foursome came together when Mr. Pagnotta hired the sisters, who had moved to New York to be musicians. (In high school, Tracy was the bassist and Tonya the drummer for a punk band called Prophylactic Fear. "Go ahead," Ms. Hurley said. "Take your time to laugh. You got to know we didn't name it. We were just the two chicks with these skinheads.")

Mr. Pagnotta and Ms. Hurley fell in love first. Soon after, Ms. Martin said, Mr. Clarke literally fell for her. Or near her. One night after an Erasure event, he was saying his goodbyes to her while walking backward. When he tripped, Ms. Martin recalled, "I said, 'Oh, my God, you love me already.' Of course, I was kidding."

Now, she said, "It's like a commune. It all blurs together. We all have our hands in each other's business."

On a family camping trip, Mr. Clarke and Ms. Hurley made a zombie movie together, using action-figure party favors, just for fun. Ms. Martin's eyes are the first to see Ms. Hurley's gothic novels: her first series was called "ghostgirl," for its deceased heroine; the new series, "The Blessed," is about a trio of martyred teenagers. Ms. Hurley has directed Erasure videos, and Mr. Clarke writes the music for her book trailers and movies.

Mr. Pagnotta, by proxy, has also contributed to the family's morbid leitmotif. The sisters' uproarious and affecting film

about his mother, an irresistible widow named Mary, follows her as she visits the grave sites of her many deceased family members, in a performance that would make Ruth Gordon proud. (It's called "So-lo-Me-O," and it aired on PBS in 1999.)

"I feel like we're so intertwined, I don't know who I am on my own," Ms. Martin joked. When Ms. Hurley left to pick up their children from school — Isabelle Rose Pagnotta and Oscar Martin — Ms. Martin admitted that she frequently impersonates her sister on the phone. It's a protective gesture, she said: "Her nervous banter can go off on a tangent." (It is the case that Ms. Hurley is more garrulous than her sister.) "I actually got her the job at Reach. I did her phone interview. I wonder if Michael knows that."

The idea for the new Morbid Anatomy Museum was planted one Halloween when Ms. Martin and Ms. Hurley attended a talk that Joanna Ebenstein was giving about the cult of Santa Muerte, or Saint Death, at a bookstore in Brooklyn.

Ms. Ebenstein, an artist, is something of a scholar of the macabre. Since 2008, she has presided over the Morbid Anatomy Library, a tiny exhibition space at Proteus Gowanus, an arts organization, that grew out of her wildly popular Morbid Anatomy blog, both of which are devoted to expressions of all that is ghoulish: books bound in human skin, for example, or post-mortem photography or Victorian mourning wreaths or Santa Muerte relics. Or, as Ms. Ebenstein likes to say, the bizarre, the liminal and the beautiful.

In this incarnation, Morbid Anatomy had accrued a passionate fan base eager to participate in its squirrel taxidermy workshops and attend its Morbid Curiosity Singles Nights. When the sisters saw the extent of Ms. Ebenstein's collections and learned her history, Ms. Martin told her, "I always thought there should be a gift shop and a cafe around this stuff." As she recalled recently, Ms. Ebenstein replied, "'You're right, and it should be attached to a real museum, and I can give that to you.'

I can't remember the moment it got serious, but it made the transition from fanciful to real pretty quickly."

For Ms. Martin, who is used to wrangling rock stars and celebrities, creating a museum from scratch was no fantasy project. She tackled it, Ms. Ebenstein said, with startling tenacity and deadpan humor. The twins will tell you they got their work ethic from their mom, a nurse who worked three jobs to raise them, with a little help from her own mother. (See "funeral fly," above.)

In just under a year, Ms. Martin and Ms. Ebenstein, along with Colin Dickey, co-editor of "The Morbid Anatomy Anthology," and Aaron Beebe, an artist and the former director of the Coney Island Museum, assembled a board, hired the executive and curatorial staff, found an architect (two, actually), raised money in a Kickstarter campaign and found space in a former nightclub in Gowanus. The Brooklyn Arts Council is a sponsor. The other day, Ms. Martin proudly brandished the museum's official charter from the state.

The three-story, 4,200-square-foot museum — painted black, of course, and designed by the architects Robert Kirkbride and Anthony Cohn — has not just exhibition spaces, but an expansive library, a lecture and events space, a gift shop and a cafe, where you'll be able to snack on mourning cookies and chocolate bird skulls. The

ABOVE: Tonya Hurley and Tracy Martin are twins who grew up attending funerals with their grandmother.
OPPOSITE: In the living room of Ms. Martin's house, Art Deco club chairs sit on either side of an Eastlake mirror, and a framed "Mourning Hair" wreath hangs over her desk.

first show was on the work of the Victorian taxidermist Walter Potter, a cult figure who made weird anthropomorphic tableaux of things like kittens getting married, having tea or playing poker. There are Morbid Anatomy residencies and Morbid Anatomy workshops — wearable taxidermy, anyone?

When Ms. Martin held a fund-raiser for the museum at her house, Ms. Ebenstein said, its décor showed Ms. Martin to be a true believer. "You can see from Tracy's house that her aesthetic is a rarefied version of what our aesthetic is," Ms. Ebenstein said. "Almost an aspirational model of what Morbid Anatomy is all about. It was really important for our community to see that. It put our cult audience at ease. I think they could see that the museum is not going to be this stupid, kitschy death-salon place."

The house enjoyed a different kind of fame when Mr. Clarke and Ms. Martin bought it from Jenna Lyons, creative director of J. Crew. Ever since appearing (twice) on the cover of the old *Domino* magazine, the place had been relentlessly blogged about. Fans pored over its elements: Ms. Lyons's bright yellow English sofa and spare kitchen, her beds with their plain white sheets, the entire bedroom she had turned into a closet.

It was also a fantasy for Ms. Martin, who had dreamed about living in a classic Brooklyn brownstone ever since she and her sister shared a one-bedroom apartment in Brooklyn Heights.

She is not alone in the fantasy. There was a bidding war, she said, and Ms. Lyons

The bedroom is painted an eggplant color from Fine Paints of Europe. The Indian four-poster bed is from the 1850s, the botanical engravings are 17th-century Dutch and the chandelier is French.

FROM LEFT: A vintage slipper chair sits next to a Swedish Baroque armoire in the master bedroom; the powder room is papered in hand-embroidered silk, and the faucet is from Roman and Williams's collection for Waterworks; the "19th-century kitchen" was designed and built by Roman and Williams.

asked that final bids be accompanied by a personal essay, just like a college application. "I wrote a really long letter," Ms. Martin said. "I told my story — we have sons about the same age — and made my case and my promise that I would love the house as much as she had."

Also, she said: "Vince ponied up. I told him, this is it. This is where I'm going to die. Hopefully not anytime soon."

With help from her sister, Ms. Martin began to fill the place. But its visual legacy — the ghost of Jenna Lyons — was hard to shake. "I kept trying to buy her sofa, but in a different color," Ms. Martin said.

She had always planned to outsource, but it wasn't easy to find designers who shared her sensibility. Finally, she saw photographs of Ms. Standefer and Mr. Alesch's own loft, a mash-up of early-20th-century industrial elements, ebonized wood, fur, metal, leather and bones. Their firm, Roman and Williams, has a reputation for making places that appear to have been around for 100 years, without looking like historical re-creations.

Ms. Standefer said: "When we first saw the house, we were like, 'Wait a minute, isn't this the J. Crew chick's place?' It was too spare and too contemporary for Tracy,

but she had no idea how to get it to the sort of maximalist, feminine place she wanted. We tend to lean masculine. We rarely get asked for more feminine elements. Embroidered wallpapers meets the toughness of buffalo hide. Awesome, we thought. Let's not taxidermy this out."

The one room untouched since Ms. Lyons's departure is the cedar-paneled basement. Real estate photos show it outfitted like a den, but Ms. Martin said it was another giant closet (the one upstairs is now the master bedroom). Mr. Clarke moved right in with his synthesizers. It reminds him, Ms. Martin said, of the cabin where he works in

Maine, and where they lived full-time when Oscar was born.

A note about surnames: Ms. Martin explained that Mr. Clarke's legal name is Martin, but he changed it when his first hit, the Depeche Mode blockbuster "Just Can't Get Enough," was released and the local newspaper published an article on the band. He was only 18, and had no confidence, she said, that "the music thing" would work out.

"He was afraid to use his real name," Ms. Martin said, "because he was afraid he would lose his unemployment benefits. He never thought he would make a living with his music. He still doesn't."

HIGH AND MIGHTY

BY JULIE SCELFO • PHOTOGRAPHS BY TREVOR TONDRO

The story of how Richard Meier, one of the world's most celebrated architects, came to design a small, one-bedroom house on a barrier island likely destined for extinction goes back nearly a half-century.

It was 1969, and Phil and Lucy Suarez were newlyweds. Mr. Suarez would eventually become the business partner of the acclaimed chef Jean-Georges Vongerichten, but at the time he had just co-founded a company that became very successful at producing popular commercials and music videos. He and Mrs. Suarez had bought their first apartment, in Gramercy Park, and were contemplating a renovation. When Mr. Suarez asked a colleague to recommend an architect, he was given the name of Richard Meier, a rising star already becoming known for his dramatic stark-white buildings.

Mrs. Suarez had never heard of him. "So Lucy calls him and says, 'I want to see your portfolio,' " recalled Mr. Suarez. "And Richard said, 'Excuse me?' "

After seeing a photograph of one of Mr. Meier's houses, though, she was astonished. "I saw this house and said, 'Oh, my God! If you can do this, you can do our apartment.' "

Over the course of the renovation, the three became close friends, a bond that endured even after Mrs. Suarez redecorated the all-white interior Mr. Meier had meticulously made for them, introducing a riot of textures and colors. ("I want you to be prepared for a little bit of a change," she told him during a strategic phone call before their annual Christmas gathering. "He said, 'You can do what you want with your house.' Then he called back and said, 'What is it you did?' ")

It was around this time that George Lois, the legendary ad man and Mr. Suarez's first boss, invited the couple to visit him in Fair Harbor, a small town on Fire Island with wooden bungalows and a bon-vivant-meets-bohemian personality. Mrs. Suarez, who has a reputation for being the last one at a party, instantly fell in love with the communal cocktails and barefoot dining.

The couple bought a bay-front summer cottage in Fair Harbor in 1971, and several years later upgraded to what was then an expensive midcentury modern house on a quieter street. Like most homes in the area, it was a wooden structure with no air-conditioning or insulation, but it had views across the bay and enough deck space for a grill and plenty of visitors. For nearly four decades, the Suarezes hosted an endless stream of friends. And over time, they purchased two adjacent waterfront houses for guest quarters, creating a small compound. "There was a lot of love in the walls here," Mr. Suarez said.

The glass-and-steel house, designed by Richard Meier, replaced a more conventional wooden structure that burned down.

That was what made it so painful when an electrical fire took down the house in 2011.

"It was 40 years of pictures, and all the tchotchkes and gifts that were given to us," Mrs. Suarez said. "Everything that was something to do with the beach, something to do with our friends."

They were still reeling several weeks later when they had one of their regular dinners with Mr. Meier and he offered to help them rebuild. That an architect who had by this time won the Pritzker Prize, architecture's version of the Nobel, and was known for ambitious projects like the Getty Center in Los Angeles would have an interest in something so small and possibly ephemeral was astounding to them.

But Mr. Meier loved the idea. After almost 50 years of practicing as an architect, it was like coming full circle: The first house he ever designed and built was on Fire Island, in 1961, for the artist and illustrator Saul Lambert and his wife. ("They had $9,000 to spend," Mr. Meier recalled. "I didn't have a lot to do in those days, so I said fine.")

Soon they were having regular meetings at his office. Mrs. Suarez told him she was hoping for something with the charm of the old wood house, but early in the process the couple was forced to confront an unwelcome reality: Because of new construction codes aimed at minimizing storm damage, the new house would have to be elevated.

As Amalia Rusconi-Clerici, one of the designers, said: "They were used to having a house that was pretty much on the ground; now you have this grand entrance that you walk up. It's a new concept we all had to accept."

Once they came to terms with that, however, the couple became more open to the idea that Mr. Meier envisioned, something entirely different from the original. But building the steel-and-glass structure he had in mind presented a number of challenges on Fire Island. For starters, they had to dig 10 feet below sea level to bury the wood piles. Then they had to put a steel frame on top that could support 25 tons of glass.

Sam Wood, the contractor, had been working on Fire Island for 30 years and had

Lucy and Phil Suarez are old friends of Richard Meier's, but still they were astonished that an architect known for large, ambitious projects would be willing to design a small one-bedroom house to replace the one they lost.

never seen anything like it. "It's built like a mini-skyscraper," he said.

"We had ironworkers on the job for two months straight," he added. "An ironworker on Fire Island? Maybe once before in 25 years we've welded on job sites here."

What's more, some of the I-beams weighed 5,000 pounds, so he had to rent a barge-mounted crane to hoist them onto the site directly from the ferry. But when the first load arrived, he discovered the bay was too shallow for the barge to get anywhere near the shore. "So one by one," he said, "we brought every single steel column from the dock up to the house by wagon and dolly."

Still, all that effort proved worthwhile. Before the house was completed, its first test arrived in 2012, with Hurricane Sandy.

And while many homes on the island were destroyed, the mini-skyscraper survived unscathed.

As Mr. Suarez put it, "If that house falls down, then literally the island is gone."

True, it is something of an oddity here, a steel-and-glass structure that sticks out among the more conventional beach houses. But maybe because of its modest size — just 2,000 square feet — or maybe because of the laid-back attitude of the community, there has been little backlash or gossip among the neighbors.

Mr. Vongerichten, a frequent guest, offered an explanation. "A lot of people who are successful have people who are jealous of them," he said. "But with Phil and Lucy, you just want to hang out with them."

Lucy Suarez regards the home's all-white color palette as an opportunity to decorate with brightly colored furnishings, like the outdoor dining chairs at right, from Paola Lenti.

COMFORT IN A LITTLE GINGERBREAD

BY JOYCE WADLER • PHOTOGRAPHS BY TREVOR TONDRO

The most magical things in life are the ones that spring up where you least expect them — the rosebush in the abandoned lot, for example, or in the case of Sandra Foster, the tiny Victorian cottage in the Catskills that shares space with a 1971 mobile home, two aged trucks, a pen full of chickens and a hand-lettered sign advertising "Farm Fresh Eggs, $2 a Dozen." The chickens and their eggs are the remnants of a restaurant that Ms. Foster's husband, Todd, a great bear of a man, tried to run in this sleepy college town last summer;

like the landscape business he started a few years earlier, it failed. Mr. Foster, who is working at a local poultry farm, suffers from back troubles, making Ms. Foster, a fiscal administrator at Brookhaven National Laboratory on Long Island, the primary wage earner.

No matter. Ms. Foster has her own shabby-chic retreat. It may not have a bathroom or a kitchen, but it is a dream of Victoriana: stacks of Limoges china with tiny rosebud patterns; chandeliers dripping crystal; billows of tissue-paper garlands.

This is all the more impressive because she renovated the 9-by-14-foot cottage, an old hunting cabin, herself.

Ms. Foster haunted upstate salvage shops from Kingston to Albany for old windows with wavy glass; she found an old porch door in the precise shade of hunter green once used on the boarding houses that dotted the area; she used a jigsaw to create gingerbread trim and cut out openings for the windows.

This is a very special sort of dream house: the Victorian Ms. Foster has wanted since she was a teenager on Long Island and her middle-class family lost their home. It is a house that is as soul-satisfying as it was when she first imagined it as a 15-year-old, even with the ups and downs that grown-up life brings.

"My refuge," she calls it.

The Fosters' country homestead is a study in contrasts, as are the Fosters. She is a size zero and wears pink wellies, black tights and a paint-spattered Irish knit sweater over a brown jersey. Sitting in their trailer, listening to her husband speak, she brushes first the long hair of Zuzu, one of

The porch: a triumph of salvage. The door is vintage; the window box was made from salvaged wood; the step (also a tool drawer) is topped with wood from a bench pulled from the creek; and the flooring was salvaged from partly rotting boards in another house.

28

Sandra Foster turned an old hunting cabin into the romantic cottage she had always wanted, using vintage columns, flooring and wavy glass windows, and doing the carpentry herself.

her two Maltese dogs, whom she sometimes refers to as her daughter, then her own long white-blond hair.

Mr. Foster is a man whose chest gives the impression that he has to go through doors sideways. An independent spirit who left high school at 15 to see the country, he has worked as a carpenter, a cook and a landscaper. His two much-larger dogs are Ruffy, a Doberman mix he found by the side of the road, tossed from a car as a puppy, and Mullet, a Labrador retriever. He also has 19 chickens, 8 chicks and 8 baby pheasants. Plus, Ms. Foster noted, two hummingbirds, though technically, they merely visit.

The Fosters' 14-acre property in Delaware County has a "Men Are From Mars" — as in, they decorate with dog hair — "Women Are From Venus" feel, although they share the trailer, which is their actual home. (Ms. Foster's romantic studio, lacking heat as well as plumbing, is uninhabitable in winter.) With its '70s-era avocado-and-gold color scheme, it is known as the Groove Tube.

Mr. Foster's personal property is his "man cave," a truck-size shed covered by an enormous tarp. It's furnished with a big-screen TV, lots of videotapes, cooking equipment and two lamp-warmed cages for the chicks and pheasants. (Note on young pheasants: They are the rare infants that are not cute. But when you are introduced to one, on someone's outstretched palm, you must pat its head anyway.)

Across a stream and up a steep hill is Ms. Foster's Victorian cottage. With lavender blush white petunias in a window box and lace curtains, it is clean as a summer cloud.

Ms. Foster's dream of a country house began when she was in high school in Holbrook on Long Island, and her father, a radio announcer, tried to start his own radio station. After the business failed, her family lost their home, and Ms. Foster said she spent "lots of my high school years being homeless," living with her family in furnished basements or spare rooms in her parents' friends' houses. (Her younger sister, Nicole Tadgell, an award-winning

children's book illustrator, remembers it as being less than a year.)

Despite the financial pressures, Ms. Foster said, her father would consider no work but radio and had difficulty working with others.

Mr. Foster, hanging near the open door of the trailer, had a thought about this. "I would suggest he probably lost a lot of his spirit, kind of felt broken," he said. "He being an entrepreneur and going through many phases of businesses opening and closing."

What was the effect of homelessness on Ms. Foster?

"If you don't have a home, you don't have a sense of place, you don't have a life, you don't have a soul," she said. "This was a nice average suburban community. We were four kids and two parents living in a single room. I got very internal. I buckled down and did my homework. I got used to living in small spaces."

Ms. Foster was an honor student in high school, then graduated from Wheaton College in 1990 with a B.A. in literature and a $16,000 college loan. Unable to find a good job in New York City, she stayed with her mother in various rental properties on Long Island and worked minimum-wage jobs to pay off her loan. For several years, she worked two full-time jobs. Her solace was listening to the band Rush and gardening, she said, but whenever the landlord wanted his house, she'd lose her garden.

It was while she was working in Suffolk County, as a mail carrier by day and sterilizing glasses for a pharmaceutical company at night, that she met Todd Foster, who was then working for a landscape company.

The attraction?

"I was a gardener, he was a gardener," she said. "There is a plant called nepeta. I had trouble growing it. He grew it like gangbusters. I was fascinated by this very handsome man who could grow something I couldn't grow like there was no tomorrow."

They married in 2000 in a Renaissance-themed ceremony ("I made 19 cloaks," Mr. Foster said) and settled in Riverhead, N.Y. A year later, longing to be

The shabby-chic retreat is a dream of Victoriana: stacks of Limoges china with tiny rosebud patterns; chandeliers dripping crystal; billows of tissue-paper garlands.

The sleeping loft is accessible only by ladder — which has kept Ms. Foster's husband, Todd, who has back troubles, from joining her there. The chandelier over the bed is from Target, as is the Simply Shabby Chic by Rachel Ashwell bedding.

The mirror was "a strange Band-Aid color — sort of pinky orange," Ms. Foster said, when she found it at a yard sale. She painted it with Ralph Lauren's Cove Point in flat white, the same color she used on the cottage walls.

The cottage fulfills a dream for Ms. Foster, whose family lost their home when she was a teenager.

in the country, they bought a big, rundown farmhouse three hours away, near Kerhonkson. Ms. Foster worked two jobs on Long Island to pay for it, going upstate on weekends, while Mr. Foster stayed at the farmhouse and tried to start a landscape business.

"This is when I discover, much to my horror, that Todd and I aren't completely alike," Ms. Foster said. "He is not a tidy man, he likes to collect things and stuff, most of which is very large, like tractors. My idea of houses is Victorian, cute, magazine-perfect, lots of white. When I come home on the weekend there are dishes in the sink, dog hair everywhere and he has probably dug some new hole with one of his excavators because he wants to put a pond in, and I have three acres to weed-whack instead of mow — on the weekend, mind you, and I'm working two jobs."

She continued: "It was horrible. I don't have the money to do the things I want to do, like decorate. We wanted to have kids, but I don't feel like I can stop working because I'm funding all this. Growing up with homelessness, I know the consequences of stopping working."

The stress became so intense that Ms. Foster had what she called a nervous breakdown: falling on the floor, screaming, crying.

"The huge house was half renovated, the life was killing me," she said. "The only thing holding me together was Todd's love, and his love of food and feeding me, and his love of flowers. Every single day I come here, there are flowers. A whole path of rose petals leading to a bath full of rose petals and candles. He's a magical man, despite his flaws."

Their great big farmhouse, they realized, was ruining their lives. Soon they found this wooded property, with the trailer and cabin, for sale. Ms. Foster, seeing the hunting cabin on the hill, knew it could be her dream house.

"It was like coming home," she said, after Mr. Foster had gone to do chores and the conversation had moved up the hill to her cottage. "I get tears in my eyes thinking about it. It was everything I had dreamed

of, in every novel I had read, every song I had heard."

The cabin was then a 9-by-10-foot box with a peaked roof, five small windows and a sleeping loft over a small porch supported by tree trunks. Ms. Foster began work on it as soon as time and money allowed.

Armed with a crowbar, hammer and electrical saw, she removed the front of the cabin and extended the floor and porch, using salvaged floorboards. She framed out the porch and found columns, a screen door and hardware at New York Salvage, in nearby Oneonta.

The only help Ms. Foster required from her husband was setting the columns and rafter over the porch. The four columns cost $60 each, and one was split lengthwise to make decorative pilasters for the porch.

Armed with her saw, Ms. Foster cut out spaces for windows, which she bought for $30 each at Historic Albany Foundation's Architectural Parts Warehouse. She found a tin ceiling on Craigslist for $200, and a wooden mantelpiece at the Linger Corner Gift Company antiques store in High Falls for about $350. Many of the faded white book jackets came from Beth Neumann, at Tattered Vintage.

Furnishings, which had to be carried across a shaky bridge over the stream and then up the steep hill, posed a challenge. So what appears to be a short, fat love seat is really a lightweight wicker sofa from Ikea, plumped up with pillows and embroidered Ralph Lauren pillowcases. Ms. Foster built the china closet using scrap wood and French doors she found at a yard sale.

Was she ecstatic when it was completed?

"Yeah," Ms. Foster said. "I was. I remember the night I finished as clear as a bell: November 1. I was listening to Rush at very high volume over and over, it was freezing cold, I was starting to paint, but the moon was out. I looked up at the moon, twirling, with my arms out. I was ready to cry."

Does she plan to install plumbing and turn it into a real house?

"Not really," she said. "It's just my little studio. If I add on to it, I have to pay taxes.

It might be nice to have a fireplace, but do I want to live with Todd up here? I would probably have to clean up after him. What's the point? It's a tale of two cities."

Ms. Foster cannot yet fulfill her dream of living in the country full time — quitting her job and trying to find another would likely mean a pay cut — so she makes the four-hour drive back and forth from the city every weekend. "You have to be self-sufficient in this world, a woman especially," she said.

Finally, it was time to go back down the hill and across the stream to the trailer, where her husband came through the door with a surprise: freshly baked rolls, still warm from the oven.

He placed them in a basket and put them, with a bucket of margarine and cups of green tea, on the coffee table. Surrounded by four dogs — two from Mars, two from Venus — everyone ate.

A stream runs between Ms. Foster's cottage and the trailer that she and her husband, Todd, live in. Furnishings must be lightweight enough to carry across.

WITHIN ARM'S REACH

BY JOYCE WADLER • PHOTOGRAPHS BY TREVOR TONDRO

Enid Woodward's toenails are painted blue, a color you don't often see on a mature woman. The walls of her tiny Manhattan penthouse are even more unusual — a strong sky blue, with blocks of red.

We are not talking pale colors here. This is color as an explosion of energy, color that could hurl you into the air if, by some magic power, color were given force: a comic-book blast of Superman blue and red. It's a bold choice, particularly since you cannot move from Ms. Woodward's blue-and-red living room to, say, a bedroom painted a tranquil

and self-effacing eggshell white. The living room is the bedroom is the dining room.

The apartment is one open space — and at 600 square feet, a very small space. And while many who live in small studios hide their beds in pull-down contraptions, Ms. Woodward does not. Her bamboo-backed four-poster stands large and proud, "a temple within a temple," as she and her design team at D'Aquino Monaco call it.

"A friend of mine came in and said, 'This is your bedroom, right?'" Ms. Woodward said. "She knew better, but she just couldn't get her mind around it."

She gestured with her hand at points about the room — the bed, the TV, the built-in desk. "I said, 'No, this is my bedroom, this is my media room, this is my workroom.' The nice thing about a house tour is you can do it standing in one place."

Ms. Woodward's voice carries a touch of her native west Texas, though she has been in New York for more than 30 years. She was a founder of a dance company, Woodward Casarsa, and worked with it for the five

years it existed in the early 1980s; she later worked as the on-tour physical therapist with the Alvin Ailey dance company for 10 years. She now has her own physical therapy office in Manhattan.

She is involved in spiritual studies, primarily Buddhism in a down-to-earth way: the advantage of cooking for people who are on a retreat in silence is that they can't complain about the food, she said. She also said that when she and her husband of some 20-odd years divorced a few years ago, they used a mediator because they were determined that their marriage would have a "graceful end."

Ms. Woodward and her former husband, a financier and real estate broker, lived in the same prewar, Upper West Side apartment house where she now lives, in a large two-bedroom, two-bathroom apartment with a dining room. They later bought the little apartment directly above them. They planned to break through and turn the two into a duplex one day. When the marriage ended, Ms. Woodward, who loved the build-

A backless Donzella Tête-à-Tête daybed keeps the 600-square-foot space open. The walls are painted Pratt & Lambert's Blue Celeste.

ing and the neighborhood, got the little apartment.

It had a cramped, dark bedroom and a tiny, walled-off kitchen. But it also had a very large asset: a wraparound terrace that was nearly the same size as the living space. Access was through a narrow living room door, though, and the terrace was only visible from two small windows in the living room, a small mullioned window in the bedroom, and another small window in the walled-off kitchen.

Still, for Ms. Woodward, who had gotten into gardening when she lived for a time in Los Angeles, that terrace was a big draw. And she was not concerned about a small living space. What was important to her was that her home be a refuge, she said, where she could decompress and restore herself.

To create that refuge, she worked with Carl D'Aquino and Francine Monaco of D'Aquino Monaco, an architecture and design firm. She gave them a few pictures she had pulled out of magazines: a cottage in England where everything was gray except for intense blue shutters; a bath house in Istanbul; Moroccan tiles.

She realized later that the team had also taken note of what she was wearing: a poncho a friend had knitted for her in burnt orange, a color that was echoed in the Burmese pots and bowls she had about the house. They had also listened carefully when she told them about her frequent spiritual retreats.

"She's a very spiritual person," Mr. D'Aquino said. "She loved color, which we love to work with; she also loves to garden and to cook."

Ms. Monaco added: "I don't remember the three images clearly other than they added up to one word — creating a sanctuary. She also had a great connection with Buddhism, and within a lot of the imagery of the Hindu gods they often use this really rich, intense blue as a background."

The renovation took 18 months from planning to completion. The wall between bedroom and living room was knocked

down, as was the wall in the tiny kitchen.

Windows were an important design element. The multi-paned window in the bedroom was replaced with a more modern single panel of glass; in the kitchen, a window was added and another enlarged, giving Ms. Woodward views of both sides of her terrace; and the living room wall adjoining the terrace was replaced with glass doors.

The cast-iron radiators dating to when the building was constructed, in 1927, were removed. In the bathroom, a new radiator was cleverly concealed in a glamorous wall of mirrored storage; in the main room, radiators were hidden behind two broad steps leading to the terrace. Those wide steps, Mr. D'Aquino said, could also serve as additional seating.

The original steel entrance door to the apartment, however, was retained. With layers of paint removed, it has an antiqued

Enid Woodward's studio may be small, but it has one very large asset: it opens onto a wraparound terrace that is nearly the size of the living space.

look that works perfectly with Ms. Woodward's collection of Etruscan pottery and handmade bronze sculptures from the Far East.

Providing the full kitchen, space for a washer and dryer, and the storage space that Ms. Woodward wanted required the kind of meticulous architectural planning found on a yacht. Her bedside tables, the desk and the kitchen cabinets were custom built. The laundry facilities, closets, refrigerator and dishwasher are all hidden behind red panels.

But Ms. Woodward and her designers decided there was one thing they did not want to hide: the bed. She and Mr. D'Aquino had independently selected the same one — a bamboo-backed four poster, the Otto Canopy Bed from Gervasoni, which was a splurge for Ms. Woodward at $5,348. Using a hideaway was never considered; for those times when an exposed bed seems too intimate, drapes can be used to divide the room.

"It's a wonderful piece of furniture," Ms. Monaco said. "It doesn't need to disappear to make a room functional."

"Who wants to come home at night and pull out a bed?" Mr. D'Aquino added. "You want to enjoy your beautiful linens. With a hideaway bed, you're cutting yourself off from that whole aesthetic, and the bed becomes something to be ashamed of."

Ms. Woodward agreed: "I knew if I did a built-in bed, it would never be in its built-in — it would just be a big old cabinet with a bed down."

The Moroccan tiles Ms. Woodward coveted line the floors of the bathroom and the kitchen and border the wooden floors in the main living space.

For help with the terrace, Ms. Woodward worked with Karen Fausch, who owns the Metropolitan Gardener. There were, Ms. Fausch says, a great variety of plants and planters when Ms. Woodward brought her in — so many that the terrace felt hectic and overwhelming. Ms. Fausch added five trees to expand and define the space, placing two crab apples on either side of the entrance, with benches and birch trees around the area for privacy.

Most of the planters were replaced with fiberglass containers from Capital Garden Products. To tie outdoors to indoors, two were finished in the same blue as the apartment walls, as were the Bryant Park garden chairs. (The garden renovation required an additional budget: Trees cost between $250 and $350 each, and planters ranged in price from $200 to $600.)

Ms. Woodward kept the long reclaimed teak table from Country Casual that was already on the terrace. She also has boxes for lettuce and a Meyer lemon tree. ("I get just enough to make one very small lemon tart or one margarita," she said.) Pine trees, which are visible from the bathroom, suggest the Japanese gardens she admires.

Like anyone who has conquered a small space, Ms. Woodward is aware of what she can and cannot acquire. She has room in her tiny kitchen cabinet for exactly six plates, six cups, six saucers, six glasses and six wineglasses, she said. And she has 12 inches of space in a closet for her "longs," so if she gets a new dress or coat, something has to go.

Is there nothing she misses in terms of space?

"No, not at all," she said. "I just feel like I have everything that I need, and I am constantly amazed at how convenient everything is. Everything just seems close at hand, because the place is so small. It seems like a great luxury to have it that way, instead of a great liability."

But Ms. Woodward grew up in west Texas, in the land of wide-open spaces. Doesn't she sometimes miss that?

"No," she said. "Where I grew up it was one line of earth and sky. And what's interesting here, there is a lot of sky and blue. You see the tops of buildings, you see sky. It's about sky."

Tiny apartments require meticulous planning. In Ms. Woodward's 6-by-7-foot kitchen, the refrigerator and dishwasher are concealed behind red paneling. But using a hideaway bed was never considered; the Otto Canopy Bed from Gervasoni is "a wonderful piece of furniture," said Francine Monaco, one of the studio's designers. "It doesn't need to disappear to make a room functional."

THE ANTI-MCMANSION

BY SANDY KEENAN • PHOTOGRAPHS BY BRUCE BUCK

Living in a one-room house with an ultra-minimalist aesthetic and two small children sounds more like the setup for a joke than something any reasonably sane person would attempt. And yet that's exactly what Takaaki and Christina Kawabata set out to do when they renovated an old house here. They were convinced that an open space with as few toys and material possessions as possible was a recipe not for disaster, but for domestic calm.

Still, living this way takes a kind of discipline that many find hard to fathom.

"Most of the people we've invited here are shocked by how we live," Ms. Kawabata said. "How we can raise kids without toys and clutter and stuff everywhere."

Mr. Kawabata laughed. "They think we're Buddhist monks," he said.

In fact, Ms. Kawabata runs a small design business called Takatina out of their home, and her husband works for the Manhattan architecture and interior design firm Janson Goldstein. And Mr. Kawabata modeled his design for the 1,200-square-foot house with its 14-foot ceilings and black-stained oak floors on communal living in 17th-century rural Japan. That, and his own childhood in a one-room farmhouse in Nakajima.

"There wasn't much in the way of heating," he said. "So my mother would be cooking and my grandmother was always knitting by the fire. That was my memory: everyone living all together in one room."

The couple decided to leave Williamsburg, Brooklyn, in 2008, because they could afford more space here. But even so, when they moved into their new home the following year, Ms. Kawabata said, "We actually threw away half our stuff."

Summing up their philosophy, she said: "We love the things that we have and try not to be wasteful. The rest, we edit."

One Saturday afternoon, their son, Tozai, poured barley tea for a visitor, and Akari, their daughter, carried pastries to the table, displaying poise and dexterity beyond their years. They also behaved like children everywhere, competing for the adults' attention by dancing, singing and showing off their drawings.

"The children are always surprising and delighting us here," Ms. Kawabata said.

Mr. Kawabata added, "Without walls, there is constant communication."

Eventually, there will be an addition, a 1,500-square-foot structure that may be connected to the main house with an open walkway. But that's a few years off. For now, instead of walls, the family makes do with transparent room dividers created out of metal frames wrapped with nylon string.

The children have a designated space for

Above the living area is an open loft where the adults sleep; below is the kitchen. Christina Kawabata had hoped for a state-of-the-art setup, but what she got was a plywood counter with painted sawhorse legs.

playing and sleeping sectioned off by one of those frames, and at the end of the day, it is their responsibility to clean up their toys and set up the futons on which they sleep. Pillows are tossed down from the parents' sleeping loft above.

"They are allowed to make a mess in their specified area — their bedroom — and every time they use their toys, they have to put them back in the bin before going on to the next one," Mr. Kawabata said. If they ask properly, are on good terms with each other and are doing well in school, he con-tinued, they can request that the toys they are using be swapped out for other toys stored in the unfinished basement.

However, Tozai has begun to realize that not everyone lives this way. His par-ents have handled the situation by repeat-ing what has become an informal family mantra: How many toys can you play with at the same time?

So far, it seems to be working.

"We're basically brainwashing him," Mr. Kawabata said. "That's how my father did it to me."

"Most of the people we've invited here are shocked," Christina Kawabata said of the home she shares with her husband, Takaaki, their daughter, Akari, and son, Tozai. "How we can raise kids without toys and clutter and stuff everywhere."

54

SLEEPING IN THE AFTERTHOUGHT

BY SANDY KEENAN • PHOTOGRAPHS BY JANE BEILES

Even before Hurricane Sandy swooped in and wiped out 15 years of her work at the Battery Conservancy, where she was director of horticulture — in charge of what she thought of as her "23-acre roof garden" — Sigrid Gray had already decided to leave the city.

Her exit also had nothing to do with the changes happening in her Williamsburg, Brooklyn, neighborhood, where she had spent nearly 25 years living in an industrial art space and managing a balky 1934 residential building nearby. Or with anything going on in nearby Green-

point, where she had assumed the (pro bono) stewardship of the grounds connected to the Police Department's 94th Precinct headquarters back in the 1990s. (The disarray bothered her trained painter's eye and Scandinavian sense of order, and when she made an impromptu offer to organize things, the desk sergeant replied, "Knock yourself out.")

Simply put, her city energy was spent.

"Changing Williamsburg amazed me, but at that point it could have been lined with dancing bears and pony rides," said Ms. Gray. All her instincts told her it was time to move on. As she put it, "I prefer open land."

Her relocation requirements were quirky and rather specific: grounds that would challenge her, with trees and distant vistas and eccentric slopes, but that wouldn't need extensive tending. And nothing terribly remote.

After a number of scouting trips, she eventually found what she was looking for in the historic district of Kinderhook, a Hudson Valley village settled by the Dutch in the 17th century. "It was a small property, but it had many planes," she said of the not-quite fifth of an acre, with a 1,500-square-foot house on it. "I knew I could garden it for a very long time."

Out front, she has planted a lawn of Canadian fescue that tops out at eight inches and needs only two trims a year. Along a side border, she is training a live willow fence in an intricate diamond pattern, and behind the house is a large slab of bluestone waiting to be chiseled into a birdbath. Half of the driveway is being ripped out so that more of her favorite things — sour cherry trees, Irish moss, blue flax, horseradish and asparagus — can take root, somewhat willy-nilly, as is her preference.

The second floor gained about 30 inches in height when the roofline was changed from pitched to gambrel. The orange chair was found at an antiques market in Stamford, Conn.

"It's got another year and a half before it all knits," she warned a visitor. "There's a plan, but I'm afraid it's only in my head."

What about the house?

To her, it was something of an afterthought, of indeterminate style and equally fuzzy vintage. At first, she didn't mind that it had exposed beams that were mysteriously not attached to the walls or that you could see through the floorboards between the first and second floors. Her plan was merely to spruce up the kitchen with new cabinets.

But James Dixon, the Chatham, N.Y., architect she hired, kept making small observations and helpful suggestions for other alterations here and there. And soon she started seeing what he saw: a house in need of a more authentic identity — and a complete overhaul.

Mr. Dixon and his colleague, Matthew Herzberg, asked her to consider changing the roofline from pitched to gambrel, to give it more presence and get an extra 30 inches

"It's an amazing experience to have a new house built around you, almost like a new skin," said Sigrid Gray of the way her architect, James Dixon, went through the house with her, reimagining it room by room.

58

LEFT: The living room sofas are from Restoration Hardware; the pillows are from One Kings Lane. ABOVE: The print over the fireplace is by Elizabeth Bramsen, Sigrid Gray's grandmother. The Shadowy chair is by Tord Boontje.

or so on the cramped second floor, a convincing argument for the 5-foot-10 Ms. Gray.

From that point on, she almost never said no to their ideas. And they went through the house, reimagining it room by room.

"It's an amazing experience to have a new house built around you, almost like a new skin," she said.

The transformation, which more than doubled the cost of her initial investment, received an award from the local chapter of the American Institute of Architects.

Everyone on the design and construc-tion team wanted her to go with a flashy front door, lobbying hard for yellow. But Ms. Gray insisted on keeping the look quiet. Every project has its star. And this one, she said, was never about the house.

"They did an amazing thing: They found grace in the house," she said. But for her, the real grace lies beyond its walls.

For the first time in her horticultural career, she said, "I now have the pleasure of waking up in the middle of my garden. There are drip lines on timers and I can ac-tually hear them going off."

The kitchen has marble counters and a subway-tile backsplash. The black rattan Storsele chair in the kitchen is from Ikea. Ms. Gray refinished the antique cherry table herself.

DOWN HOME, BUT OUT THERE

BY PENELOPE GREEN • PHOTOGRAPHS BY ROBERT RAUSCH

Like a medieval village, Butch Anthony's 80-acre family compound is a self-contained universe, and every inch of it is an expression of his prodigious creative spirit. It makes a tempting destination for folk art aficionados, as well as the sort of art world tourists who've already ticked Marfa, Tex., or Joshua Tree, in the California desert, off their lists.

Mr. Anthony, a lanky and laconic man who dresses exclusively in Liberty denim overalls (he owns 25 pairs) and a battered straw hat (he has 10), is a self-taught artist, builder and local hero, whom the state of

Alabama once chose to make a Christmas tree ornament for the White House — the Bush 43 version. He is also the host of the Doo Nanny, the annual alt/folk art "micro" festival, as he calls it, that started as an "art party" he and two friends gave on the side of the road in nearby Pittsview, and eventually moved to Mr. Anthony's property here.

"There's a 100-foot vagina we're fixing to burn," Mr. Anthony remarked while filling a garbage can in the back of his battered truck with water, a precautionary measure, one gathered, in case things got out of hand.

But why a vagina? "They've got a burning man, why not have a burning woman?"

Like Burning Man, the extreme art fair held each summer in the Nevada desert, the Doo Nanny offers both a burning effigy and an exercise in creative camping. Mr. Anthony

has thoughtfully provided a tepee, an outdoor kitchen, a solar-powered shower, outhouses and a wood-fueled hot tub, all built from and decorated with the sort of handmade trash-into-art pieces — ethereal chandeliers pieced together with cow bones and twigs gnawed by beavers — that are his specialty.

It now attracts an intrepid crowd of makers and their fans who gather on the last weekend in March not only to show their work — and sell some, too, if they're lucky — but to hang out with like-minded friends and partake of Mr. Anthony's particular brand of Southern hospitality, which is certainly as homespun and country as his accent, but has an impish, renegade backbeat.

It is also a chance to see Mr. Anthony on his own, very atmospheric, turf.

His compound, which once belonged to his grandfather, a cotton farmer, is now

Butch Anthony began building his log cabin in 1988 and is still tweaking it. He made the chandeliers on a screened porch from twigs and cow bones.

Mr. Anthony describes his art, which includes old family portraits (not his own) embellished with skeletons or creatures of his own imagining, as "intertwangleism." His definition: "Inter, meaning to mix," he said, "and twang, a distinct way of speaking. If I make up my own 'ism,' no one can say anything or tell me I'm doing it wrong."

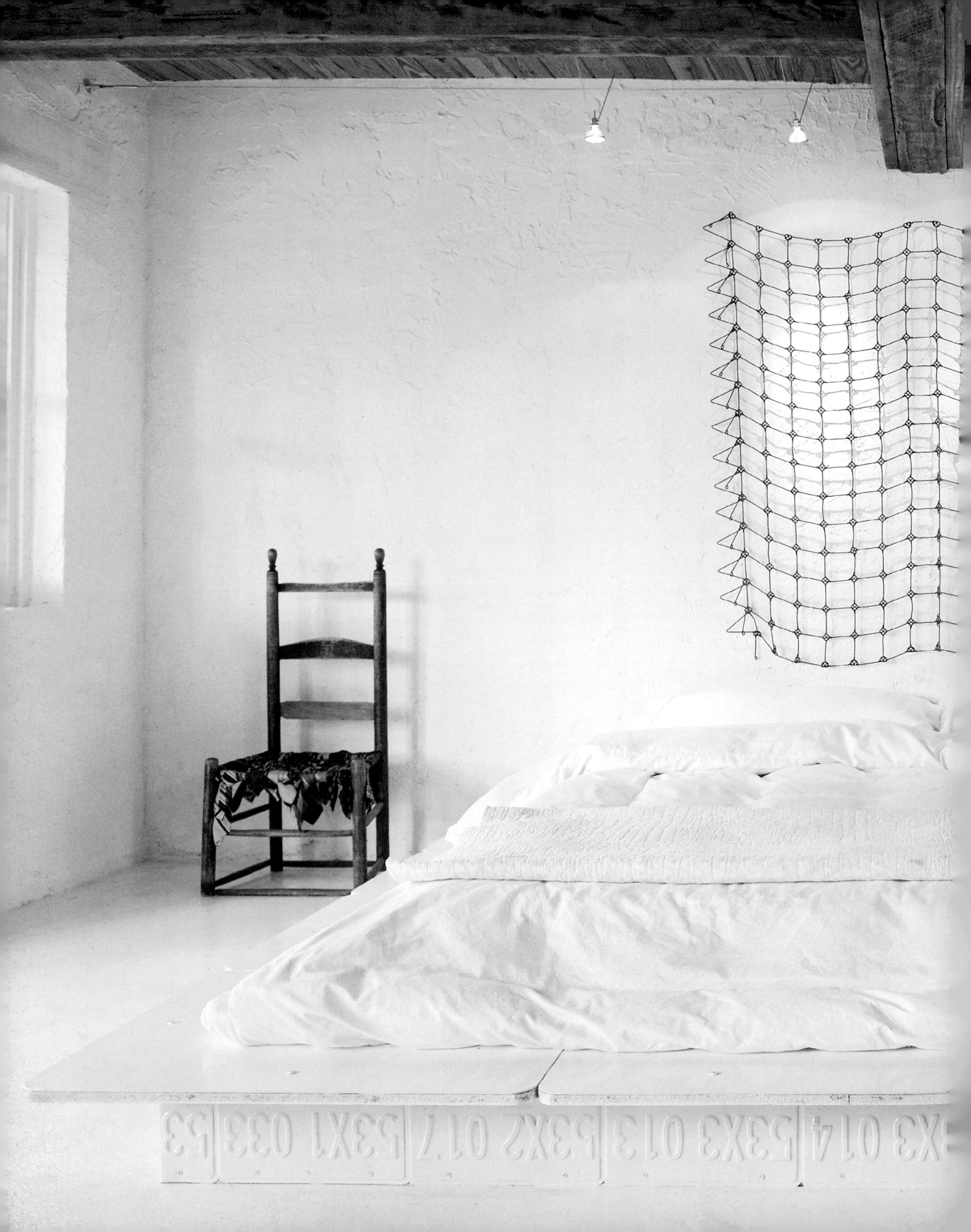

home to Mr. Anthony; his father, Bishop Anthony, a retired insurance adjuster and occasional restaurateur; and sometimes Mr. Anthony's partner, Natalie Chanin, and their daughter, Maggie. (She and Maggie come and go "on a part-time basis," Ms. Chanin said, because her business — producing handmade clothes and soft goods under the Alabama Chanin label, which is sewn by local seamstresses and coveted by fashion world insiders — is run from her own home in Florence, Ala., a five-hour drive away.)

Other permanent residents include two peacocks, three chickens (Bob Ross, a blind 21-year-old white-crested Polish show rooster with a gift for fortune-telling, passed on), four dogs and a cat. A tiny dancing donkey named Soapstick lived here, too — a You-Tube video showcases his talent — but he kept escaping, and Mr. Anthony got tired of chasing him, so he gave Soapstick away.

Les Blank, the documentarian with an appetite for American originals (he has made films about Dizzy Gillespie and Alice Waters), has been filming Mr. Anthony.

When will the movie be done? "That's a good question," said Mr. Blank, who described Mr. Anthony as a kind of "national treasure."

In any case, there's much to see here, including the one-room log cabin Mr. Anthony built at 14 and the log house he began in 1988 and is still tweaking, made from heart pine salvaged from an old mill and put together with the help of his homemade rigging — cables and pulleys strung from the branches of pine trees. There are fields of artwork — like Dia: Beacon, but rural Alabama-style — that include enormous "bowls," woven from beaver sticks, cow bones and old shoes spray-painted white, and scraps of metal Mr. Anthony weaves together with hog wire to make siding, a material he has used in projects for the Rural Studio, the Auburn University architecture program that creates innovative housing for Alabama's poorest residents.

A truck ride away, but still on the property, is the Possum Trot, a barbecue restau-

RIGHT: The bathroom next to the bedroom has "windows" made from "beaver sticks," a k a twigs chewed by beavers. **ABOVE:** Inside the twiggy bathroom.

rant and junk auction house run by Mr. Anthony and his father, which comes to life Friday nights. The auction proceeds benefit the bands Mr. Anthony invites to the Doo Nanny. "Maybe someday we'll make some money," he said.

Finally, there is the Museum of Wonder, a barnful of curiosities — the "world's largest gallbladder," a replica of a human skeleton, a stuffed chicken — and more of Mr. Anthony's artwork, which includes 19th-century portraits painted over with crisp white images of skeletons and old photographs affixed to paintings of mythical creatures of his own imagining.

Like many contemporary artists, Mr. Anthony concerns himself with taxonomies, exploring questions of identity — familial, racial, biological and so forth. Unlike most contemporary artists, he was educated not at art school but in the woods here, where he skinned snakes, hunted raccoons and alligators and dug up arrowheads and fossils. (His alligator-hunting technique: Jump on their heads from above, so they don't have time to swim away.)

He did study zoology at Auburn — having dug up a Mosasaurus vertebrae at 14, he had made friends with paleontologists there — but dropped out his senior year, stymied by a required public speaking class. "I've always been nervous about crowds," he said. "That's why I live in the woods."

"The art thing," as Mr. Anthony likes to say, began in 1994 and can be summed up with this oft-told tale: John Henry Toney was then a local tractor-for-hire. Plowing Mr. Anthony's garden one day, he unearthed a gnarly turnip with a human countenance and made a drawing of it. As a joke, he and Mr. Anthony stuck it in the window of a friend's junk shop with a $50 price tag, whereupon it was scooped up by Scott Peacock, the Atlanta-area chef and longtime collaborator of Edna Lewis, dame of Southern cooking.

"I thought, 'Hell, if John Henry can sell one, I'll try too,'" said Mr. Anthony, who embellished a "motel" painting — a cheap still life — "with a scraggly old paintbrush and some old paint set" bought at a Possum Trot auction. Not to be outdone, another

friend, James Snipes, known as Buddy, began bringing his creations to the same junk store; they, too, sold briskly. Thus, three careers were launched.

Mr. Snipes, who paints on twisted roots, twigs or tin, and Mr. Toney, who makes gentle, allegorical colored-pencil drawings on cardboard, fall more easily into the outsider art category; Mr. Anthony's work is harder to categorize.

Fred Fussell, a former curator at the Columbus Museum in Columbus, Ga., and now an independent curator and writer who focuses on traditional Southern culture, described Mr. Anthony as "one of a number of what I would call eccentric artists, which just means he does his own thing and doesn't have much connection to other things except himself. I don't like the term 'outsider.'

"In a whole number of ways that derive from his highly creative imagination," Mr. Fussell continued, "he comes up with innovative thoughts and processes. He breaks down whatever he's rendering into these various parts that are part physical and part invented by him. His is a really nice way of looking at the physical world."

Mr. Anthony has made up his own word, "intertwangleism," a label he paints on a lot of his pieces, which he defined this way: "Inter, meaning to mix," he said. "And twang, a distinct way of speaking. If I make

ABOVE: The kitchen is heated by a wood-burning stove. The mantel was salvaged from an old house being torn down nearby. RIGHT: Mr. Anthony wore out three chainsaws slicing the lumber for his house, which is fitted together with dovetail joints.

up my own 'ism,' no one can say anything or tell me I'm doing it wrong."

Before the turnip incident, Mr. Anthony had been making a living selling barbecue lunches to the crew at the local paper mill. Making art quickly became more appealing. "In the food business," Mr. Anthony recalled, "everyone was always complaining — the food's too cold and whatever — but the art people were treating me like a king."

The Doo Nanny began as a "little art party" with Mr. Toney and Mr. Snipes in Pittsview, the town where their friend had his junk shop. Mr. Toney named it, Mr. Anthony said. "He'd say, 'When are we gonna have that Doo Nanny again?' "

At the festival, Mr. Toney and Mr. Snipes are elder statesmen, courtly and serene among the gamboling art students. In contrast to the young folkies' rainbow garb, the two look elegant in plain overalls: Mr. Snipes was in denim, Mr. Toney in brown Carhartts and a black felt fedora.

Recalling his turnip epiphany, Mr. Toney said: "I started drawing, and I haven't stopped. I always felt like that turnip meant something, but I couldn't tell you what." (The turnip now lives under glass, like the Mona Lisa, in Mr. Anthony's Museum of Wonder. It looks like a fierce, bristly elf.)

Ms. Chanin, helping Mr. Toney find a glass of water for his "seizure" medication, grinned.

Mr. Toney continued: "Butch makes me think about Samson and the jawbone," referring to the biblical tale of Samson slaying an army of 1,000 with a donkey jawbone. Then he stumped off through the woods, leaving a reporter to wonder if he was simply noting Mr. Anthony's habit of using bones in his work, or speaking metaphorically.

Ms. Chanin and Mr. Anthony met at an art show and pig roast at the Rural Studio in Newbern, Ala. With her silver hair and her silver-haired wolf dog, which had accompanied her, Ms. Chanin "really stood out," Mr. Anthony said.

She was struck by the similarities in their work. His stitched metal siding, she noted, was like a crazy quilt. They made a promise to trade artwork. She stitched him a shirt, and a year later, he appeared at her home "with a whole mess of art," he said, "and one thing just led to another."

On their second date, Ms. Chanin came to Seale. "Butch had said he lived in a log cabin in the woods," she said, "but this was like a vision."

On their third date, they visited a sacred Native American site, a healing wall built by a friend of Ms. Chanin's, which also featured a fertility object, a stone that Mr. Anthony "was nonchalantly tossing around and making jokes about," said Ms. Chanin, who steered clear of it. Nevertheless, their daughter, Maggie, was conceived.

"That was a shock," said Ms. Chanin. Born on the first day of spring, Maggie is heir to the Doo Nanny, as some guests pointed out.

The flaming vagina went off as planned, ignited by a "meteor" constructed from twigs and old ties. The bonfire burned for hours, roaring on the edge of the pond. There were no injuries, though earlier Mr. Anthony had punctured an ear drum cutting brush, mashed his thumb with a hammer and sliced the bridge of his nose.

"The Doo Nanny can be dangerous," he said.

Mr. Anthony is not technically accident-prone, Ms. Chanin suggested, "he just gets carried away."

She added proudly: "Butch can work wood or metal, he can grow anything. He has an incredible way with the things of the world, whether it's a tree or a piece of junk, and he has his own aesthetic about how it should go together. He knows the name of every leaf and every plant and which ones you can eat. And if the world ever came to an end, I would want to be by his side."

On Friday nights at the Possum Trot auction, Mr. Anthony and his father serve dinner to the auction-goers. Mr. Anthony's "intertwangled" art is for sale there, too.

CAPE OF MANY COLORS

BY SARAH SAFFIAN • PHOTOGRAPHS BY TONY CENICOLA

Eliot Angle's favorite spot in the getaway that he and his wife, Alexandra, designed has to be the outdoor shower. "Sure, the weather makes it a little challenging to use at times," he said, noting that 100-mile-an-hour winds and driving rain are not unheard of here, even in the summer. "But the romantic rusticator in me sticks with it." (For the less adventurous, there is a 1920s footed bathtub indoors, bought and refinished in nearby Halifax.)

Inspired by local barns, with a nod to the spare Scandinavian aesthetic, the Angles' 2,400-square-foot shingled cottage is all about the outdoors. The windows frame views in every direction: Cape Breton Highlands National Park to the north, the Gulf of St. Lawrence to the west, forested hills to the east and headlands to the south. And the landscape dictated the way the house looks inside as well.

The Angles, interior designers who live in Los Angeles, took long walks, photographing the densely wooded terrain in different seasons — the changing colors of the spruce, pine, birch, maple and cedar trees, and the goldenrod, rosa rugosa, blueberries, raspberries and cranberries.

"We designed this house based on the color palette of the land and sky," Ms. Angle said. "There are 10 different shades of blue, gray and green."

A lobster crate–style deck wraps around the exterior; inside, a channeled window seat — her favorite spot — spans the width of the living room. Built by a local car upholsterer, it is covered in spruce, celadon, ice blue and lavender cushions. Green pots and chartreuse goblets sit on the open shelves in the kitchen, over blue-gray cabinets. The maple floors are all stained white.

Northeast Maine was where the couple had intended to build a vacation home, but in 2006, after deciding that the area was overdeveloped, they headed up to Nova Scotia, where they fell in love with the region's most remote corner.

"Cape Breton is sort of the next Maine up the coast," Mr. Angle said.

Ms. Angle added: "Your closest neighbor is half a mile away. I love that feeling."

Their plans for the 54 acres they pur-

Eliot and Alexandra Angle, interior designers from Los Angeles, fell in love with Cape Breton Island, where they built a house inspired by local barns. The wind, often fierce, is sometimes calm enough that the couple's daughter, Elefe, can fly a kite.

The 1920s bathtub, with its view of the Gulf of St. Lawrence, is one of Ms. Angle's favorite spots in the house. The Piet Boon desk was imported from Amsterdam. OPPOSITE: Ms. Angle designed the plywood bed; the ceiling fixture is antique. A side table is made from driftwood.

chased were initially much grander. Working with an architect, they conceived what Ms. Angle describes as "a wildly impractical fantasy": a sprawling glass-and-steel structure with a sail on the roof, the kitchen and bedrooms in separate buildings, and a central deck.

"The sail would have ripped in a week," she said. "The glass would have blown in."

Plan B was to buy a 19th-century Presbyterian meeting house with 50-foot ceilings that they heard about through an architectural salvage company, and transport it 50 miles, from inland Nova Scotia to their coastal hilltop. "It was a glorious space," Mr. Angle said. "And we liked the idea of reusing this abandoned structure."

The contractor nixed that idea. With the high winds, he told them, it would collapse in a year, if not sooner — possibly while he was putting it up.

By now, the Angles were starting to feel not just overly ambitious but also self-conscious. "Our land is in a prominent place, the highest point around," said Ms. Angle, who imagined their new neighbors thinking, "Oh, my God, these people fly in from L.A. and throw up this huge steel-and-glass house, or this 50-foot-tall church."

So, over a bottle of Glen Breton, the local single-malt whisky, at a waterfront pub, they sketched out ideas on napkins,

coming up with a plan for a more modest house that would complement, not compete with, the environment. The two-story, two-bedroom, two-bath structure, made of local birch and maple, was completed in 10 months, and the Angles spent their first summer there in 2009, with their daughter, Elefe, and their Tibetan terriers, Sturtevant and Augustus.

Although the Autoban Octopus chandeliers were imported from Turkey, the Gio Ponti Superleggera dining chairs are from Italy and Ms. Angle's Piet Boon desk is from Amsterdam, many of their furnishings are of the region: Several pieces are from antique shops in the area; Mr. Angle built an end table out of driftwood found while beachcombing; and Ms. Angle designed a hooked rug with a pattern inspired by the region's underwater plant life, working with local women who make rugs for lighthouses and fishing boats and who jokingly call themselves "hookers." "Sailors used to while away the hours working on these rugs together," Mr. Angle said. "It's a great old tradition."

The house isn't finished yet — the Angles plan to break ground on a second structure with guest quarters and an office for Ms. Angle — but the gradual pace suits them. "Unlike projects for clients, when I have a year to be 100 percent done," Ms. Angle said, "this one can take time."

The windows frame views in every direction: Cape Breton Highlands National Park to the north, the Gulf of St. Lawrence to the west, forested hills to the east and headlands to the south.

THE LOFT THAT MEDIABISTRO BUILT

BY PENELOPE GREEN • PHOTOGRAPHS BY TREVOR TONDRO

In 2007, when Laurel Touby, the freelance writers' saloniste, sold her online media company, Mediabistro, for $23 million, she banked a little more than half that amount and looked forward, she said at the time, to having a new car with a driver, a new apartment and a whole new life. Two out of three of those things, she quickly learned, are what a payday like hers buys you in Manhattan.

She is still driving her 2002 Subaru Forester. Instead of a new car, Ms. Touby acquired a $30,000 handwoven leather, chain-mail and fur

indoor swing designed by a guy who also works in anthracite, a medium Ms. Touby and her husband, Jon Fine, a musician and magazine writer, found a little grim for their taste. The swing was one of the first things they chose for their new apartment, a 4,000-square-foot loft a few blocks north of Union Square — "in the heart of Silicon Alley," Ms. Touby will tell you proudly.

Ms. Touby's policy regarding her affairs is relentlessly open kimono. "I have no boundaries and no taboos, and I figured once it was public, why not talk about it?" she said, referring to the sale of her company. "I wish when I was growing up people had been more honest about things like money."

To learn how to handle her windfall properly, she and her husband made a list of "smart rich people," like Tony Greenberg,

a serial entrepreneur, and grilled them on topics like charitable giving, requests from family and friends, and how to allocate their resources.

Famously brash and bossy, Ms. Touby charged her decorator, Jaqueline Touby, a distant cousin whom she met by accident when she moved to New York after graduating from Smith in the 1980s, with making a place "that everyone would be jealous of." SHoP Architects, creators of the Museum of Sex and the Barclays Center, gutted and rebuilt the loft in shiny surfaces: stainless steel, lacquered walls and glazed concrete.

Choosing and then waiting for the sort of art furniture Ms. Touby and Mr. Fine were after, like a black rubber Harry Bertoia chair, takes buckets of money and time. Mr. Fine said they quickly went beyond what he used to call in his younger days "Design

The spalted maple chairs and walnut slab table were made by John Houshmand. The kinetic light sculpture was designed by Jaqueline Touby.

Not Really in Reach" (though amid so much custom work there were some relative bargains, like $3,500 for a plastic-and-glass coffee table filled with cobalt-blue pigment and a toy taxi that was a copy of an Yves Klein piece). Months can stretch into years. To be sure, in the middle of it all, there was a yearlong sabbatical during which the couple took a modern grand tour, though Ms. Touby regrets its timing because she found the renovation so invigorating.

When the final piece was installed — a blush-colored ceramic chandelier — and Mr. Fine had returned from the last concert of his reunion tour with Bitch Magnet, the post-punk, hard-core, Oberlin-grown band of his youth (and about which he wrote a memoir for Penguin), the couple had a housewarming party. They invited more than 200 friends and colleagues, former employees and former bosses, along with the concrete pourers, stainless steel fabricators, lacquerers and cabinetmakers who worked on the apartment, as well as some emerging artists whose work was also displayed, albeit temporarily (and quietly for sale).

"It was superb," Ms. Touby said later of the party. "I wanted it to go on forever."

The event marked a milestone in Ms. Touby's 20-year career — a midpoint, she hopes, as she is reimagining herself as a venture capitalist — as does the apartment it was held in.

Diminutive in stature only (Ms. Touby is 5-foot-1), this Miami-born entrepreneur has a Bildungsroman familiar to even casual observers of the New York media scene, and to almost anyone who regularly reads Web sites like Gawker. For Ms. Touby has been accruing snarky (as well as grudgingly admiring) ink since she started a monthly series of networking parties for writers and editors at an East Village bar in the early 1990s.

The self-described "desperate freelancer" used to cold-call magazine editors, who were baffled by her intentions. "Who are you?" they would ask. "Who do you represent?" Then she would strong-arm them into attending her events, which she presided over wearing a brightly colored feather boa and two-tone glasses.

"I was a party dominatrix," she will tell you, who herded shy young writers into groups and forced them to talk to one another. Lonely and single and still new to New York, Ms. Touby had this idea, she said, "that I could meet editors at The New Yorker and date one of them. I had multiple ulterior motives."

ABOVE: Laurel Touby and Jon Fine spent three years renovating their Silicon Alley loft. LEFT: Mr. Fine's office has a 1960s Danish desk; he pruned his collection of vinyl and books before they moved in.

It wasn't long before she realized she could use the Internet, then in its infancy, to invite people to her parties, as well as much more: Create an online platform for job listings and offer publishing classes, health insurance for freelancers and actual content, like media commentary to rival Gawker's. Martin Peretz of The New Republic was an early investor. Cyndi Stivers, the founding editor of Time Out New York who is now editor in chief of The Columbia Journalism Review, sat on Mediabistro's board.

Yet Ms. Touby remained a media outsider, a role she welcomed and still flaunts. While her peers were mocking her as a networking freelancer, no one seemed to realize that Ms. Touby was actually something else: a natural entrepreneur.

"She made herself into a bit of a personality with the boa and the glasses," recalled Alan Light, a music journalist and former editor of Spin and Vibe magazines. Mr. Light attended a few of her parties when he was the young editor in chief at Vibe in the early '90s. "She wasn't hiding behind any pretense, however. She was pretty upfront about what it was all about. In a world that's as cool-obsessed as most of the media world is, it's not hard to figure out why people were ready to not take her all that seriously. I'm not surprised that her success brought out the snark."

Ms. Stivers said: "Way before anyone else, she saw there was a market for niche online classifieds. On a certain level, she did it instinctively. She also had a really good eye for talent. She spotted Brian Stelter when he was a college student. She spotted Rachel Sklar." Mr. Stelter is now a business reporter at The New York Times; Ms. Sklar is a media blogger and CNN contributor.

"The feather boas distracted a lot of people from the person of substance," Ms. Stivers added. "It seems to have been a reason for people to dismiss, overlook and underestimate her."

Of course, as Ms. Stivers went on to say, on a certain level being underestimated can be an advantage. Remember that Ms. Touby was building her company during the dot-com boom. While other dot-com entrepreneurs quickly found themselves trophy apartments to swan about in, Ms. Touby, Ms. Stivers said, "stayed in her one-bedroom on Avenue A and got the job done."

Mr. Fine and Ms. Touby met at a media conference in Arizona in 2002 when he was a columnist at *Ad Age*. He was charmed by her forthrightness. Pointing out the difference in their ages (Mr. Fine is five years younger), Ms. Touby told him if he wanted children in 10 years they had better not date. (He told her he could add.)

She thought he was cute, but a player, the guy who hits on all the girls at the conferences. He also exhibited ruthless networking skills. In one exchange, Ms. Touby recalled, "where I was oversharing my fears to him, he looked past me, said, 'I have to talk to that guy,' and ran away. I was devastated. I truly thought I had seemed too insecure and thus he was exiting stage left."

Today, the two bicker gently and happily. She calls him a peacock; he admits to being a "clothes geek" and claims to have taught his wife to dress properly.

On a tour of the apartment and all its

The first thing Ms. Touby and Mr. Fine bought for their new apartment was a hand-woven leather, chainmail and fur hammock designed by Jim Zivic. ABOVE: Jaqueline Touby designed this copy of an Yves Klein original; Laurel Touby added the toy taxi.

In the bedroom, shiny lacquered walls and a bed with drawers from Karkula. Ms. Touby and Mr. Fine bought the "Love" pillow in Paris; they also have "Hate" pillows from Jonathan Adler. ABOVE: The bathroom has a steam shower and a tub built for two.

pricey fixings (that sprawling sectional sofa cost more than $30,000), you ask the couple if it makes them anxious to live with so much high-end gear.

"I was brought up to worry about stuff," said Ms. Touby, who was raised by a single mother and described her childhood as chaotic. "So I'm anxious all the time. We're both pretty anxious people."

Still, they seem to be having fun, like children left home alone by the grown-ups. They have fantasy bathrooms: There's a disco ball in one that was designed like an '80s fantasy lair, with mirrored finishes that evoke Halston on a cocaine bender, and a steam shower and tub for two in another.

There is so much storage hidden behind the shiny walls that Ms. Touby hired an organizer to provide, as she put it, "a taxonomy of things," so that she and Mr. Fine could figure out what to put where. In the kitchen, drawers sport labels like "Whisks," "Graters" and "Peelers." Mr. Fine said he had the organizational skills of a goldfish, as well as a large sneaker collection, so he was doubly grateful for the assistance.

Their resources have given them dependents, like Ms. Touby's mother, but there is pleasure in that, they said. They are also helping to put seven nieces, nephews and cousins through college.

Some mornings, Mr. Fine said, they wake up expecting someone to throw them out of their fancy-pants loft. "If so, I'd still feel lucky," he said. "I was looking for Laurel for a very long time."

As for Ms. Touby, her anxieties transcend the price of her furniture, she said. When pressed on what she spends time worrying about, she answered quickly.

"Losing it all," she said. "Or being forgotten."

THE BAREFOOT CHATEAU

BY ELAINE LOUIE • PHOTOGRAPHS BY ANDREA WYNER

La Socelière is proof that a man's castle can also be a home. The 17th-century chateau is so down-to-earth, in fact, that all four generations of the Laviani family go shoeless when they visit in the summer: Giuseppe and his wife, Giacomina, who bought the place in 1999; their children, Ferruccio, an architect based in Milan who is known for designing the 2003 Bourgie lamp, among other things, and Clara; Clara's husband, Antonio Fontana, and their two daughters, Marta and Giulia; and Marta's daughter, Anita, the first great-grandchild.

The first day you're there, Ferruccio Laviani said: "Maybe you feel a little down, far from the real world. The mobile phone doesn't work well. The Internet goes jumping. The TV channels to see are just five instead of the millions. But when you start to get used to it, you begin to learn to lie down on an armchair and open a book."

He continued: "I fall asleep on the couch while I look out the window at the blue pure sky, and feel light breaths of fresh air coming from the half-closed shutters. I go along the Vendée River with a small rowing boat, or I find my sheep, especially the ram, Lambert, who is like a dog running to make me a party when I arrive."

It wasn't their intention to buy a chateau. They wanted a house on the Riviera, but the Côte d'Azur was "too expensive for what you got," Mr. Laviani remembers his father saying. So friends took them to see a fixer-upper in the Loire Valley.

"When we crossed the threshold of the property the first time, we were catalyzed by the beauty and proportions of the house — she was beautiful, perfect," he said. "Then we started to look into details. The roofs of the towers were collapsed. The rainwater that entered had created problems with the structure of the floors. The interior was decorated in a very cheap way. Electrical and water had to be redone. Heating existed in only half the house."

Nevertheless, the family loved the 9,000-square-foot home and its nearly 20 acres of forest, gardens and pasture. The senior Mr. Laviani bought it and restored it.

His son oversaw the project, working with various family members who agreed on what needed to be done: "Give dignity back to the house without overdoing it," as

La Socelière, a 17th-century chateau in the Loire Valley, is 9,000 square feet. The bust in the entry hall is gypsum with a faux marble finish; the floor is white Loire Valley stone and black slate.

Mr. Laviani put it. "The main thing was to make it ours as much as possible, to feel at ease, as if it was something that had always belonged to us."

First, they brought in carpenters, electricians and painters from Italy. Then came the furnishings: a mix of Italian and French antiques collected over the years and a few 20th-century sofas and chairs. Some pieces were valuable, like an 18th-century Savonnerie rug, but others were from flea markets. The humble is mixed with the high-end and "the layering creates an intimate place," Mr. Laviani said. "If we had furnished the house in a 'style,' the result would be fake and showy."

Everyone now has a favorite room. Mr. Laviani's is the Salotto Rosa, the former dining room he uses as a studio. His mother prefers the living room, where she does her mending on a purple sofa that sits on the Savonnerie rug.

As for the older Mr. Laviani, he likes to nap on a chaise longue in the corner of the living room overlooking the back park, where he can keep an eye out for cows or sheep ambling by.

"If the sheep are coming by, it's because they are making a disaster and are eating up all the plants and the flowers," Mr. Laviani said. "And my father screams."

Ferruccio Laviani oversaw the restoration, working with various family members who agreed on what needed to be done. He is known for designing the 2003 Bourgie lamp, among other things.

The breakfast room has a Carrara marble mantelpiece. Italian XIX Empire gondola chairs surround a walnut table. The chandelier is 19th century.

"The main thing was to make it ours as much as possible," Mr. Laviani said, "as if it was something that had always belonged to us."

A SOFT LANDING

BY PENELOPE GREEN • PHOTOGRAPHS BY BRUCE BUCK

In Mongolia, felt-making is a communal affair: Women and children beat freshly sheared wool with sticks and sprinkle it with water, then horses drag it through a field. It's a centuries-old tradition that takes hours, sometimes days, considerable skill and much hoof- and manpower.

On Crosby Street in SoHo, the felt-making conceived of by Dana Barnes is also a communal affair, though she could really use a horse or two. Ms. Barnes is on her fourth washing machine — her version of galloping Mongolian equines is the hot-water cycle of a front-loading

washer, and she's not quite satisfied. "They keep locking up," she said of the machines. "I'm wondering if they have a child-sensor alert and think the wet, heavy wool is a child that's crawled inside."

Dana Barnes is a fashion designer — a Seventh Avenue veteran who has designed collections for sportswear companies like Elie Tahari, Adrienne Vittadini and Tommy Hilfiger — who has lately turned to textiles, felt rugs in particular. Ms. Barnes's felt-making is a homegrown adventure that started several years ago with a simple problem: how to cover the vast expanses of her 3,250-square-foot loft to muffle the pitter-patter of her young daughters' feet.

Late 19th-century warehouse lofts like the one she shares with her husband, Dale Westhoff, and their two daughters, Ruby and Clio, are typically hard to soundproof. Inevitably, once the girls were old enough to scamper, the downstairs neighbors began complaining.

Ms. Barnes had always loved felt, and had been playing with it on a small scale, fusing chiffon and wool to make ruched garments and scarves. (You don't need horses for delicate items like these: Ms. Barnes sprinkles unspun wool and chiffon with hot water and soap and then rolls it in bamboo shades, using an old-fashioned crafting technique to create a couture item.) Could she make a felt rug, she wondered, that was big enough — say, 17 by 25 feet — to cover the floor?

One steamy Sunday, her solution, and all it has inspired, was on display in the bright, open loft.

There were fat crocheted granny squares the size of sea turtles drying in the sun that was pouring into the living area. There were bumps of felted, braided unspun wool, Ms. Barnes's riff on a traditional braided rug, plumped up into floor cushions. There was a felt "bowl" as high as your knees. And underneath it all was the original rug, an oatmeal-colored lawn made from panels of felted batting — squares of unspun wool — that she and the young crafters and artists she employs had sculptured and then sewn together by hand.

An empty loft on Crosby Street inspired Dana Barnes, a fashion designer who is now making textiles, to create giant felted objects to soften the space.

It was a sensuous landscape of felt. You just wanted to lie down and roll around on it.

Ms. Barnes has a serious felt fetish: In her bedroom are felt masks she made to block the sun that comes through the skylight over the bed, as well as his-and-hers felt slippers. "Dale never wears his," she said.

She has also made a felted garden for her daughters' dollhouse and a felt curtain for her bathroom that looks like the flaps in a car wash. "It's the most fun I've had with any textile," she said. "We just get crazy with it."

Or as Megan Novak, one of three women helping Ms. Barnes, put it, "It's great to just come in and bust out some squares."

That Sunday, Ms. Novak was in her felting gear, a long blue gingham halter dress and a white cotton organdy apron. Without the apron, she said, it's a lint fest: "The fibers need something to slip against."

Upstairs in the studio, Ms. Novak grabbed a black organdy bag and a sack of roving — fluffy, unspun merino wool — and took it out to the roof terrace to begin crocheting. "She always does it outside in the sun," Ms. Barnes said, shaking her head. "We don't know why she doesn't get hot."

Four hours later, using a fat dowel stick and her own hands, Ms. Novak had produced an emerald-green square, about

112

LEFT: A banquette is covered with Japanese saki-ori — indigo-dyed traditional work wear — that Ms. Barnes collected on travels to the Far East. Felt discs recycled into a bolster looked like stacked shells. RIGHT: A felt "sculpture" on the wall above the kitchen area looks like a blueprint. Ms. Barnes embossed it with objects like the letters from an antique sign.

114

3 feet by 3 feet, like something made by a Brobdingnagian grandmother. She tucked it deep in the black organdy bag, cinched the drawstring and slid it into Ms. Barnes's washing machine, where she would keep watch over it for the next hour or so.

The agitation is what causes the wool's fibers to mash and separate, but sometimes the squares fall out of the bag and shred, which may be what breaks the machines. "The problem is my husband keeps buying the best ones," Ms. Barnes said dryly. Mr. Westhoff grinned and ducked his head.

It was Ms. Novak, an artist who has worked in knitting stores, who helped Ms. Barnes create the pattern for her giant granny squares. "I just love the idea of giant pieces," said Ms. Barnes, who was inspired by the afghans her mother and grandmother made in Atlanta while she was growing up. She described a creative family: Her father, an educator, built tree-houses and playgrounds for his two daughters; her mother hand-painted the wallpaper in their suburban house. "My mom and pop made everything," she said.

After figuring out, through much trial and error, how to make the rug that covers the loft's floor, Ms. Barnes began embossing the felt. She molded the wet wool over objects like letters from antique signs, bowls, anything with an interesting shape.

Up in her studio, the bulletin board is pinned with fat yarn samples, a delicate smocked dress and a collection of old corkscrews, whose shapes might find their way into a rug, she said. "When we were embossing, we were looking for new shapes," she said. "With felt, you can do anything."

The granny squares came next, and then the braided rugs.

In the beginning, they were all intended for the loft, a rough space that was a working garment factory before Ms. Barnes and Mr. Westhoff bought it nearly a decade ago. "It took a long time to make it a home," she said.

After Ruby and Clio were born, Ms. Barnes dialed down her fashion work so she could spend more time with them. Mr.

Westhoff, an aerospace engineer who had spent 20 years in finance, including as a senior managing director at a major investment bank, took an early retirement when he was 49. Both wanted the opportunity to focus on their children.

"I missed out on so much," Mr. Westhoff said. "You don't realize it until you start taking your daughters to school."

Meanwhile, the loft was coming together. With its whitewashed brick walls and wide open spaces, it presented a decorating challenge, particularly for Ms. Barnes, who is not overly fond of furniture.

Indeed, besides the felted pieces, there's not much in the loft. There's a "gathering" table, as Ms. Barnes calls it, that's a massive slab of claro walnut just 14 inches off the floor, custom-made by BDDW, the furniture store down the block. There's also a wooden egg you might sit on, three wooden cubes and a white leather platform. "That's a couch," she said, referring to the platform. "There's usually a bolster you can lean on."

"Our life has evolved around the space," Mr. Westhoff said. "It's a very casual, laid-back way. The girls can stand on the egg, do shows on the cubes. If we have a party, everything gets tossed or stacked."

He continued: "When my parents come,

Ms. Barnes's felt-making began with a familiar urban problem: how to soundproof a 19th-century warehouse loft. Solving that problem has been "the most fun I've had with any textile," she said.

they aren't happy about it. We do have chairs, but they still complain, 'It's too low, I can't get up.' "

As more felted objects began colonizing the space, visitors — friends, the parents of their daughters' friends, artists who were making pieces for the loft — encouraged Ms. Barnes to make more pieces, or asked for pieces for their own homes.

Jim Zivic, a designer and artist who was making a stitched leather rug for Ms. Barnes, was so inspired by what he saw when he delivered it, she said, that "we just lay down on the felt and started brainstorming." The two have an idea for an entire room made of felt, in which even the furniture is covered.

"I had been thinking about Turkish interiors," Mr. Zivic said. "You walk into these old palaces, and there's no furniture. That's nice. Dana and I thought to build platforms everywhere, and just have cushions and felt."

Mr. Zivic, a much-collected designer who sculpts coal into tables and makes benches out of cotton bales, is a kindred spirit.

"Someone once told me that artists think in a circular way, meaning one thing leads to another and it all comes back to this interesting first idea," he said. "Dana is a prime example of that. As soon as I walked in, it was like we had been having a conversation for five years. I just think she's a really talented person and she's energized by material in the same way I am. It's cool that she's so obsessive about felt."

Traditional textiles were an earlier obsession, said Ms. Barnes, who has collected Asian pieces for years. She and Mr. Westhoff married in Nepal in 1996, and have traveled extensively in the Far East.

"Dana always meets the artisans wherever we go and brings stuff home," he said. "I think, 'Why is that even interesting?' When we get it home, I can see it. She makes you see it."

Ms. Barnes made banquette cushions out of Japanese saki-ori — indigo-dyed work clothes — and wrapped the leftovers around a giant steel spring. This reporter

sat down on it, thinking it was a bench.

"It's just a sculptural thing," Ms. Barnes said. "I thought it looked neat."

A colorful pile of woven clothing in a corner came from Hmong farmers, she said, explaining that she had traded Mr. Westhoff's T-shirts and sunglasses for the pieces on a recent trip to Vietnam. "Look at this hat, isn't it great?" she asked, holding up a striped cap. "I just love it."

Mr. Westhoff said, "I really loved my sunglasses."

When the granny square in the wash-

ing machine was finally ready, Ms. Novak hauled it up to the roof and laid it out on cheesecloth, using straight pins to block its shape. She and Ms. Barnes began manipulating it with huge curved needles, puffing up the fibers and arranging it just so. "I want it to look alive," Ms. Barnes said. "Lofty and beautiful."

She was on deadline, creating squares and other pieces for the International Contemporary Furniture Fair at the Jacob K. Javits Convention Center, and for BDDW, which sells her pieces. Her collection,

Souled Objects, includes felted interpretations of traditional craft techniques like macramé, crochet and smocking; prices range from $95 to $200 a square foot. (A three-foot granny square — Ms. Barnes prefers the term "crocheted square motif" — is $1,575.)

"This is the next adventure," she said, though she is still pining for that horse. "Imagine if I only had a horse to pull the pieces along the cobblestone streets of Crosby — I could produce the perfect level of agitation to replicate the Mongolian felt."

LEFT: The bed is covered with a felted blanket. ABOVE: The embossed felt rug was made by molding wet wool over bowls and other circular shapes; the shower curtain is made of felt strips.

HOUZZ PROUD

BY STEVEN KURUTZ • PHOTOGRAPHS BY MATTHEW MILLMAN

Most people who undertake a home renovation will endure varying degrees of financial strain, not to mention the twisting of the stomach that happens when their dreams are slowly crushed by reality.

Adi Tatarko and her husband, Alon Cohen, experienced all of that, as well as the usual "War of the Roses"-type discord. But for them, the most difficult thing was communicating their ideas to an architect.

After struggling to describe their vision, they were told to buy books and shelter magazines, and to clip photos. But "that wasn't efficient at all," Ms. Tatarko said, because "we couldn't find enough images to show them what we wanted."

So this being Silicon Valley, in 2009 Ms. Tatarko and Mr. Cohen, then a technology director at eBay, created an online platform to solve their problem — a site called Houzz that would showcase the work of architects and other design professionals, so that home renovators would have access to lots of images from which to draw inspiration.

They asked a few Bay Area architects they knew to upload their portfolios; soon designers in other cities were following suit. Three years and two rounds of financing later, Houzz has become one of the largest resources for house porn anywhere, a Web site and iPad app that connects architects, contractors and interior designers with homeowners renovating or building a house. More than 65,000 design professionals across the country have uploaded 365,000 photos and counting, creating an almost endless flip book of English country kitchens and Mediterranean bathrooms, organized into a database searchable by filters like style, color, materials and geographic area.

Houzz's founders, whose affectionate bickering suggests a dot-com Lucy and Desi, sat in the backyard of their airy, almost fully remodeled home one sunny day in February, and explained how it all began with their move to Palo Alto.

"So we wanted to move to the Bay Area," Mr. Cohen said.

"Alon wanted to move to the Bay Area," Ms. Tatarko corrected.

"I wanted to move to the Bay Area," Mr. Cohen backpedaled.

"I wanted to stay in New York because I wanted to work on Wall Street," Ms. Tatarko said. "You see who wins."

Mr. Cohen smiled. "Ask everyone else, they'll tell you a different story."

What neither disputes is that not long after moving, in 2006, they bought a 1950s-style ranch house that needed major work.

"What we got was a house from 1955 — period," said Ms. Tatarko, a no-nonsense

Whimsical wallpaper in the bedroom softens the home's midcentury modern aesthetic.

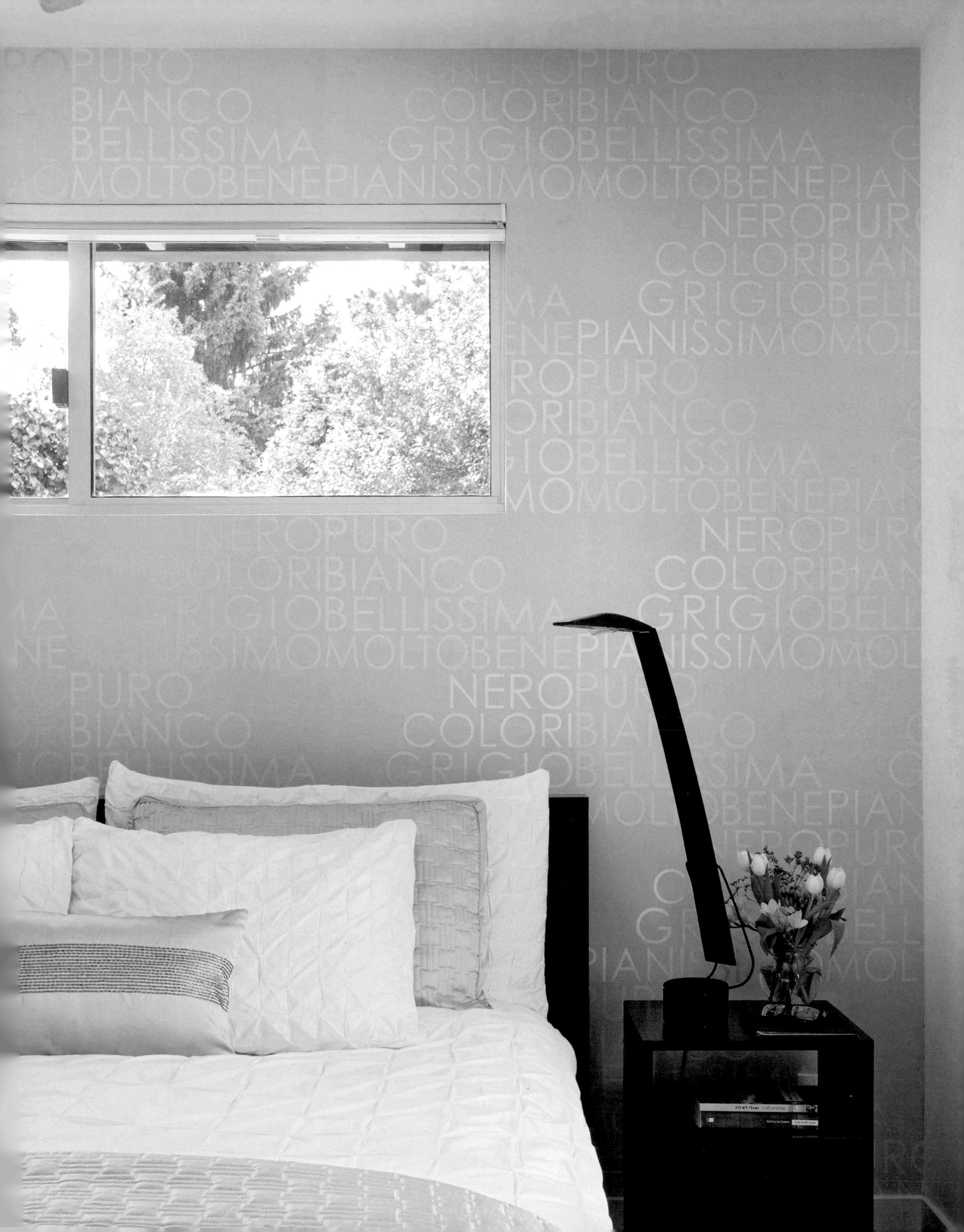
NEROPURO
COLORIBIANCO
GRIGIOBELLISSIMA

Alon Cohen and Adi Tatarko, the founders of Houzz, transformed a typical 1950s house with small, dark rooms into an open, light-filled living space. Ms. Tatarko likes fanciful interiors with pops of color, like the orange footstool in the living room.

businesswoman who previously worked for several tech companies, both with her husband in their native Israel and in New York. "The kitchen, the bathroom — nothing had been updated."

They may speak the language of home renovation now, but initially Ms. Tatarko and Mr. Cohen struggled. For three years after moving in they barely changed a bulb, making do with the small, dark rooms, an ugly dropped ceiling and a pink bathroom to save money. "Budgets are very important in a renovation," Mr. Cohen said. "Maybe for people involved in the Facebook I.P.O., money is not an issue, but for most people it is."

During that time, the couple searched for an architect sympathetic to their vision and tried to clarify just what that vision was, because Mr. Cohen likes stark, modern spaces, while Ms. Tatarko favors more fanciful interiors. "We thought it would be fun," Ms. Tatarko said of the renovation process. "Then we faced reality."

Eventually, they found an architect they liked and settled on a plan. Then, for three months, while the main living spaces were being done, they lived in the bedroom wing with their sons and went without a working kitchen.

"People ask us if it's hard to work together," Mr. Cohen said. "We tell them it's nothing compared to remodeling."

Now, of course, they have the resources of their Web site to draw on. Like other Houzz users, they can create "idea books" with photos that designers have uploaded and e-mail their "design dilemmas" to the Houzz community to get advice from professionals and homeowners. Leading a visitor through

124

The couple don't always see eye to eye when it comes to their own house. Mr. Cohen prefers a minimal look, like that of the open kitchen. Ms. Tatarko wanted an ebonized floor, though it's impractical. The bubble chandelier was an idea she got on Houzz.

their home, with its big, open living area and wall-length sliding-glass doors, Ms. Tatarko and Mr. Cohen pointed out ideas that came from Houzz, like the ebonized floors in the living room and the bubble chandelier above the dining room table.

When their son decided he no longer wanted to share a bedroom with his younger brother, Ms. Tatarko told the boys to look at Houzz and choose the colors they wanted for their new rooms. And for the master bathroom, they hired a local designer they found through the site to consult on the fixtures and colors (white cabinets and tiles in a shimmery metallic shade).

"This house is an ongoing project," Ms. Tatarko said, explaining that the bathroom was finished only the week before. "Because we

run Houzz, we don't have time to deal with it."

The company now has a staff of 26 who work from a small office in downtown Palo Alto, in a space that was once a server room for Google. Houzz secured $11.6 million in additional financing, and it partnered with Lowe's on a kitchen giveaway sweepstakes and to provide content for the Lowe's Web site.

Some have complained that the Houzz site is visually cluttered and hard to search, and that it's geographically limited (while it's mainly confined to the United States and Canada, the site has started to add international cities like London). Still, the Houzz iPad app, which has been downloaded more than a million times, is a thing of beauty — a streamlined, highly addictive

delivery system for design addicts. "Whenever we have a rough day, we just look at the reviews of the app," Mr. Cohen said, adding that the goal is to make the Web version just as user-friendly.

Despite Houzz's increased exposure, however, its founders have largely stayed in the background: There are no "Tips from Adi and Alon" or photos of their home on the site. "It's not about us," Ms. Tatarko said. "We wanted to create the right platform for everyone to mingle, no matter what their style, their budget."

The site seems to be encouraging them to take on additional renovation projects rather than bringing an end to the work — something other Houzz users have experienced as well. On the short list is an update of their home's 1950s-era exterior, new landscaping and the construction of a guest bedroom.

"We have over 800 options to find an architect in the Bay Area now," Ms. Tatarko said. She and her husband are also creating idea books on Houzz, presumably making it easier to agree on a plan and communicate with whomever they hire.

It was suggested that the renovation process might have been smoother had Mr. Cohen been the type of husband who defers to his wife on design matters.

"Adi wasn't that lucky," Mr. Cohen teased.

"That's true," Ms. Tatarko said. "But I'd rather live with somebody who cares than somebody who doesn't care."

Mr. Cohen laughed. "Now she's saying that."

THE INSTANT HEIRLOOM HOUSE

BY JOYCE WADLER • PHOTOGRAPHS BY TRENT BELL

One never forgets one's first summer love. Sherry Lefevre's was named Rosemary. She was 10 when she first encountered it — a house built in the early 1800s on Nantucket, where it is customary to give houses names.

Its furnishings were from another era: horsehair sofas with stiff velvet, threadbare Oriental rugs. Ms. Lefevre's bedroom under the eaves had a tall, dark chest with an array of things on top she had never seen before: a china perfume tray, a monogrammed dresser set, a box of collars. There was also a mysterious upstairs bedroom, accessible only through a bedroom her parents used.

At school, back home in Philadelphia, Ms. Lefevre was immersed in the literature of the 19th century — Hardy, Brontë, Melville. In this house, it was easy to believe she was part of that world. She imagined stories from the house's past, that the back staircase led to "an insane wife, hidden away, her meals smuggled up the stairs," as she writes in a book she hopes to publish.

Ms. Lefevre would have loved to inherit such a house (an heirloom house, as she calls it), full of well-loved antiques, but Rosemary was a rental. Three summers and it was gone.

Then Ms. Lefevre, an assistant professor of writing at the University of the Arts in Philadelphia and a mother of two grown children, came into an inheritance and was able to buy her own old house on Nantucket. Within a few months, she writes, she turned it into an instant heirloom house, filled with the sort of memorabilia that might have been passed down for generations: seashell art pieces, seascapes, converted whale-oil lamps, antique fabric drapes, bureaus and beds sweetly hand-painted with clutches of faded flowers.

Ms. Lefevre estimates that the cost of furnishing the house was about $15,000. There have been some concessions to comfort (no horsehair sofas). But overall, the furnishings are worn, weathered, redolent of seasons past.

"Why did my family's summer house have to be old?" Ms. Lefevre writes in the manuscript she is calling "The Nantucket House That eBay Built." "Because Rosemary was. Because I wanted a house that contained layers of memory, making it as otherworldly as summer. Because the nau-

Sherry Lefevre, a writing professor in Philadelphia, bought a 19th-century house in Nantucket and furnished it with vintage finds from eBay. The home was once owned by Samuel Robbins, a first mate on a whaling ship who died at sea in the 1820s.

seatingly maudlin motto of 'The Velveteen Rabbit' is true more or less: to become real, a house needs to show some wear, some shabbiness, some misshapenness, some evidence of love and life."

And while Ms. Lefevre's heirloom house is filled with other people's summer vacation mementos — their discarded souvenir plates, their Nantucket lighthouse postcards — that does not lessen the power of the items for her.

"There is something in particular about summer that is poignant, because we all know that when we are in summer we are in a fleeting moment that will become part of memory," she was saying one steamy day on Nantucket, when thunderstorms threatened, but thoughtfully held off until day's end. "Memory in summer is always stronger because we need it to get through the rest of the year. You know what I mean? For me, getting things that are old or things that remind you of everyone else trying to hold on to the good life makes everything kind of deeper."

Ms. Lefevre is a trim woman, friendly, articulate, sometimes quite funny. She slaps together a sandwich for a guest in the offhand

The island in the kitchen was once a counter in a store in Chicago; Ms. Lefevre paid $700 for it. She refused to spend more than $200 apiece for her Oriental rugs or paintings. Lamps could not be more than $50 each.

manner of a woman who has made thousands of summer sandwiches for children while dealing with more important things: figuring out the next semester's teaching plan, perhaps, or how she will pay the bills.

When it comes to telling her life story, she is guarded. "I don't want this to be a psychological profile," she says early on.

But on the subject of summer houses and their influence on the families that spend time there, she is happy to talk. Her childhood sounds happy. Her father was a lawyer; her mother, a homemaker. Ms. Lefevre, one of four children, attended what she describes

as a prim girls' school in Philadelphia.

One of the great pleasures of her childhood was the house called Rosemary, which she can recall down to the smell.

"It was very musty," she says. "It smelled of the sea. It basically rambled, but in a wonderful way. It had an old kitchen that was very haphazard, with curtains instead of cabinet doors. The floors in the place were just totally wonky. They were like being in a heaving ship. So we used to roll things like little trucks and see how fast they would go from the living room, downhill to the kitchen, downhill to the laundry room."

She continues: "I do think certain houses get inside kids. They live half in fantasy anyway. Though I never was in a house that had that kind of atmosphere. It stayed with me forever."

Ms. Lefevre was educated at Princeton, then Columbia, married, taught in Lebanon for a time, then divorced and returned to Philadelphia, where she raised her children, Michael and Callie, on her own. Life as a single mother was not easy. For a while, she was an adjunct professor at three different colleges, teaching days, nights, summers. Nantucket, where her parents had bought a modern ranch house on three acres with an ocean view in the 1970s, was a respite.

After her parents sold the house and divided the money among Ms. Lefevre and her siblings, she began a search for her own home on the island. Her children were growing up, and she wanted a house that would create memories for the families they would one day have, as Rosemary had for her. She also realized that one sure way to see more of your adult children was to buy a vacation home.

She was looking for an old house that had not been gut-renovated, one that retained its history. She found a house in town that, she later learned, had been owned in the 1800s by a man named Samuel Robbins, a first mate on a whaling ship who died at sea.

She paid the asking price and brought in her Philadelphia carpenter, Pat Clark, who lived there while he worked. Renovations included installing two bathrooms, removing a wall between the kitchen and a den, and putting in additional walls upstairs.

Finding the right old furnishings was

essential. Ms. Lefevre had discovered eBay only a few years earlier, when a nephew had his heart set on a particular toy.

"It was a gorilla that sings, 'I don't want to work, I just want to bang on my drums all day,'" she says. "It cost me $10, and it made my nephew more happy than I could have imagined. Then I realized, anything that you hadn't seen for so long that you missed, anything you remembered as a kid, you could get on eBay.

"When I was a kid, my brother had given me a rubber cigar that, when you blew on it, a worm popped out at one end. So I went on eBay and typed in 'rubber cigar worm,' and there it was. And it was one of those crazy moments where you say, 'Oh, my God, everything that has been lost to me can be recovered.'"

What Ms. Lefevre remembered and missed was the kind of house we were sitting in, she is told.

"Yeah," she says. "It was a big version of a cigar with the worm coming out. A very expensive version. Too bad I didn't quit when I was ahead."

Ms. Lefevre bought furnishings for her house in an organized way. She is an academic, after all. She started by writing down her associations with Nantucket and other seaside resorts. She gave herself guidelines: bedside tables and bookcases could not cost more than $100 each; rugs could be no more than $200; lamps could not be more than $50 (not including the conversion kits for the whale-oil lamps, which were about $12).

She discovered ways to find things she could afford. Visit homes on Nantucket, she says, and you will find that owners with deep pockets have a fancy painting of a ship. But

Most things in the house are old, even if they are made to measure from old fabric. One exception is the mattresses, which are all new.

a 19th-century painting like that could cost several thousand dollars. Seascapes without ships in them, she realized, were much cheaper: most of hers cost $200 or less.

Ms. Lefevre also longed for sailors' valentines from that era, framed shell compositions often containing hearts and flowers. Online, she found them for $3,500 to $18,000. But when she typed "antique shell art" into eBay's search engine, she found she could buy seashell art and objects for less than $100.

Whenever she could, she picked up furniture herself, instead of having it delivered, to reduce shipping costs. Sellers along Interstate 95, her route from Philadelphia to New England, were preferred, and she quickly discovered that better deals could be found in Rhode Island than in Connecticut.

Her big-ticket items were a $700 counter for the kitchen and a seascape for $500. (It doesn't have a ship, but it was signed by the artist Alex Mortimer.) She also found a portrait of a prosperous-looking fellow for $200 and pretended he was the deceased whaler who had once owned her home — whom she promoted to captain.

Not everything was bought on eBay. The faded flowered sofa and matching chairs in Ms. Lefevre's living room are from the vacation house of Gerry Sills, the mother of a friend. And the mattresses are all new (she paid $1,100 for four, at a furniture outlet in Morgantown, Pa.). But most things are old, even if, as with the drapes,

Ms. Lefevre amassed a collection of Nantucket souvenirs, many of them found for little money on eBay. Shell art objects, in particular, were very affordable. BOTTOM LEFT: She likes to pretend that a portrait she bought for $200 on eBay is the whaler who once owned her home.

they are made to measure from old fabric.

She has found she enjoys the personal nature of eBay shopping — the stories of the people she deals with online and of the objects themselves. On the dining room wall, there is what appears to be a homemade version of a sailor's valentine under glass, with tiny shells set in dried clusters of seaweed. Ms. Lefevre bought it on eBay for $125.

"I had this very funny experience," she says, taking the piece down and putting it on the table. "I made an arrangement to pick it up on I-95, on the way here. The owner said, 'Call me when you hit exit such-and-such,' and I met her in the parking lot of a supermarket. It was like a drug deal. I opened my trunk, and she opened her trunk. I didn't want her to ship it. I think this is old and real."

It certainly seems old. The seaweed looks as if it could turn into dust if the glass were removed. The inscription, in gold-colored ink, is so faded that only part of it is legible. Ms. Lefevre and the reporter study it, trying to decipher it.

"Call us not weeds, we are flowers of the sea, for lovely and gay tinted are we," she reads. "And quite independent of sunshine and showers. Then call us not weeds, we are ocean's gay flowers."

The story of the sailor who bought it, of the person he gave it to, is unknown. But it may be something about which Ms. Lefevre's grandchildren, yet unborn, will dream.

ROLL OUT THE SNOW CARPET

BY RIMA SUQI • PHOTOGRAPHS BY TREVOR TONDRO

"This is where we want to be" was the first thought that Clay Heighten and his wife, Debra Caudy, had when they stepped off the plane at the Jackson Hole Airport. As Dr. Heighten said, "Those mountains really make an impact."

Dr. Heighten, a physician-turned-entrepreneur, and Dr. Caudy, an oncologist, live in Dallas with the youngest of their four children (the other three are grown), and were in town visiting a business associate of Dr. Heighten's who had built a house with an enviable view of the

mountains. But then, Jackson is virtually surrounded by mountains — the Teton Range to the west and the Gros Ventre Range to the east — so it's hard to avoid having a spectacular view.

It wasn't long before they were looking for a house of their own here. Despite the recession, however, inventory was low and prices were not. "We saw a lot of tired log cabin homes," Dr. Heighten said. "And none were what we wanted."

What they wanted was a house that took full advantage of the outdoors. What they got was one that did that to an extent that may have surprised them. But then they took the unusual step of delegating almost all the decisions to their designer.

After buying a five-acre lot in 2011, they more or less turned it over to Larry Pearson of the Pearson Design Group in Bozeman,

Mont., whose firm had a 5,400-square-foot home built and furnished for them in just 16 months, Dr. Caudy said. "Larry really just sort of took over this whole house," she said. "We let him have the control."

To the extent that they gave Mr. Pearson direction, Dr. Heighten said, it was limited to general requests. "We wanted the home to blend with the outside," he said. "We wanted to be able to leave the doors open, and walk in and out. And have living areas outside."

Mr. Pearson took them at their word. And in place of a formal entry hall, he substituted an outdoor room. Of course, it has a fireplace, something that comes in handy when the weather is frigid and the snow is knee-deep, as it is in Wyoming during the winter. And there are sliding barn doors in case it gets too windy, which isn't uncommon either. But what's a little discomfort when you're

Architect Larry Pearson took his clients' requests for outdoor space seriously. "I decided to make the entry to the home an outdoor room," he said, "rather than a porch or foyer."

An Era sofa from
Camerich sits on
a 16-foot-square
sheepskin rug.
Random Lights from
Moooi hang over a
custom-designed
black walnut stump
coffee table.

The Claro walnut
bed was custom-
designed. A fuzzy
Cortina chair from
Refuge sits beside
a Modo desk lamp
by Jason Miller for
Roll & Hill. In the
bathroom, Ronbow
round ceramic sinks
with Purist fixtures
from Kohler sit on
Calacatta marble
counters. The Bella
Modern Pendant
Light is from Niche.

146

surrounded by this kind of beauty?

As Mr. Pearson pointed out, "The entry actually has the best view in the whole house."

It also has a floor that's often covered in snow, but that doesn't seem to trouble his clients. Then again, they moved in last fall, so this is their first winter, Dr. Heighten said. "We don't have that much experience."

He added: "I think in January and February, we won't use that front area that much. But we've been out there in late October, when it was 25 degrees. And we had a fire going and the blankets, and it was great."

The furniture was chosen to withstand the elements, although he said that he and Dr. Caudy do bring the cushions and the pendant light in when they're not here.

For her part, Dr. Caudy seems philosophical about the challenges of outdoor living in Wyoming. "The home is art, in and of itself — that's what people say: It's a piece of art," she said. And "of all the rooms, people love that front deck."

Clay Heighten, a physician-turned-entrepreneur, and Debra Caudy, an oncologist, live in Dallas with the youngest of their four children; the house in Jackson is their vacation home. The hanging fixture just inside the front door is a Random Light by Bertjan Pot for Moooi.

SURPRISES IN TWO DIFFERENT BOXES

BY ELAINE LOUIE • PHOTOGRAPHS BY BRUCE BUCK

If Isabelle Péribère were to articulate her philosophy of design, it would sound something like this: "I like design that surprises you as much as it eases your eye, like what looks like tile but is a wallpaper," she told a reporter recently. "People are afraid of using wallpaper because it can be bold. But it is more a piece of art, and I use it as an accent only."

What else?

"I like out-of-the-ordinary light fixtures carefully placed, like a pendant that is not centered on a ceiling, but rather tucked in a corner, to create a more interesting spatial experience."

Ms. Péribère was the chief operating officer of four Lignc Rosct stores (two in Manhattan, one in Miami and one in Philadelphia) and before that worked for Dassault Systèmes, a French company that makes 3-D software of the sort that Frank Gehry used to design the Guggenheim Museum in Bilbao, Spain. But last year, she went out on her own, starting an interior design firm. And among her first projects are the homes in Miami and Hoboken, N.J., that she shares with her husband, Jérôme Péribère, the chief executive of the Sealed Air Corporation, both of which show her love of the intentionally off-kilter.

The house in Miami, a 6,000-square-foot modernist concrete-and-glass structure on Biscayne Bay, was a collaboration with Max Strang, an architect who practices in Florida and Colorado. He was the one who gave the house its windowless stark-white facade facing the street, so that most of the views from inside are of the water. On the bay side, the house is almost transparent; many of the rooms have floor-to-ceiling sliding-glass doors, and some have glass balconies as well. (It's impact-resistant glass, designed to withstand hurricanes.)

"I wanted a wow effect — the view of

TOP: The house Isabelle and Jérôme Péribère have in Miami is a modernist concrete-and-glass structure. BOTTOM: In Hoboken, their home is a 19th-century brownstone. But both homes have modern kitchens with Bazzèo cabinetry.

152

The couple spend part of the year in Florida, where they have a minimalist house on Biscayne Bay. The master bathroom has an Almond bathtub from Porcelanosa; Marcel Wanders's Skygarden light is suspended off-center above it.

the water — as soon as you walked in," Ms. Péribère said.

The interior design, which she was responsible for, is done in a palette of grays, she said, "because I was looking for this soothing atmosphere and the elegance of neutrals."

But most rooms have an element of surprise. As she put it, "I like sleek, contemporary design with a twist of the baroque, or drama, or the unexpected or slightly out of place."

That could mean visual surprises like a brilliant red light fixture in a dark gray hallway or trompe l'oeil wallpaper (but never on more than one wall).

The house in Hoboken couldn't be more different. Or more strikingly similar.

A 19th-century brownstone, it overlooks a quiet garden, and the light, even on a hot, cloudless day, is softer and more muted than that of Miami. The Péribères bought the house and gut renovated it with Jensen Vasil, an architect in Hoboken.

Although it is a historic building, Ms. Péribère created a decidedly modern interior, juxtaposing large-scale modernist furniture with the delicate moldings, stained-glass windows and Victorian mantels. And again, there is a lot of gray, with charcoal paint on the trim and the doors. But there are also splashes of color throughout and unexpected touches like an oversize lamp suspended off-center in the living area and a taxidermied antelope with its head turned

OPPOSITE: The open living space in Miami has poured concrete floors and Fandango pendant lights by Danny Fang for Hive. ABOVE: Togo chairs and ottomans from Ligne Roset provide casual seating in the movie room.

quizzically at an angle, as if startled by one or more of the decorative choices.

He isn't the only one who was taken aback by some of the Péribères' decisions. Their Miami architect, for one, couldn't believe that such a modern couple didn't want a king-size bed. "When I was designing the house in Miami," Mr. Strang said, "I was always sketching a king-size bed for the master bedroom, but the couple kept insisting on a queen-size bed."

The explanation turned out to be a surprisingly old-fashioned one: Mr. Péribère spends nearly half the year traveling for work, but he and his wife make an effort to spend every weekend together. And as they told Mr. Strang, "We're still very much in love."

160

The master bedroom in Hoboken is furnished with a Lorraine caned bed from Restoration Hardware; Belgian chandeliers hang at different heights on either side. A 17th-century Louis XIII desk sits in a corner of the bedroom with a 19th-century French industrial chair.

THEY SHOOT POTATOES, DON'T THEY?

BY PENELOPE GREEN • PHOTOGRAPHS BY LAURE JOLIET

It was a typical weekend at the Chao Pound, to use the name Stephen Chao, the former television executive and National Enquirer reporter, has given to the six little 1920s Sears kit houses (plus barn) that he and his girlfriend, Rachel Mansur, a handbag impresario, call home.

For a few days in late June, Units H, I and J were occupied by Theo Richardson, Charles Brill and Alexander Williams, the alt-elegant, Brooklyn-based furniture designers known collectively as Rich Brilliant Willing. The three were in town for a design fair, thereby displacing Kurt Andersen, the magazine editor turned novelist and public-radio host, in town for a business meeting, from his usual berth in Unit H. So Mr. Andersen was sleeping in the cast-iron Murphy bed in Unit A.

That Saturday night was typical, too: Ms. Mansur, a designer educated at the Rhode Island School of Design (Messrs Richardson, Brill and Williams were classmates), cooked for a spicy mix of architects, furniture designers and comedy writers, including some early "Simpsons" staff members. The RBW trio hung their pendant lights from the trees in the courtyard, and there was beer and Champagne in galvanized tubs. Before long, the potato launchers came out, exhaling spuds into a brick wall in a volley of satisfying splats.

"It's like summer camp, but much more fun than any camp I ever attended," Mr. Andersen said. "It's a lovely land of make-believe that has no connection to the way L.A. is trying to be make-believe."

Part family compound (Mr. Chao's mother and stepfather live half the year in Units J and I; his two grown sons come home to Unit A), part creative commune, the Chao Pound brings an urban connectivity to the sprawl that is Los Angeles County.

Mr. Andersen and his wife, the writer Anne Kreamer, were on the phone recently to evoke its gestalt, which Ms. Kreamer likened to a Gilded Age camp in the Adirondacks or an artists' colony like MacDowell. "It's this bohemian Eastern environment," she said. "With this atelier spirit of invention and curiosity, and a constantly changing cast of characters."

Ms. Kreamer and Mr. Andersen have known Mr. Chao since their Harvard days,

Part family compound, part creative commune, the Chao Pound — where Stephen Chao, left, and Rachel Mansur live — brings an urban connectivity to the sprawl of Southern California. Built in the 1920s, six Sears kit houses form a courtyard; when Mr. Chao bought them, the courtyard was open to the street and the neighbors were in the habit of treating the place like a public park.

though they didn't kindle a friendship until he was running the USA Network a decade and a half ago and Mr. Andersen was hired as a consultant. They have been regulars in Unit H, while Mr. Andersen and Mr. Chao collaborate on television projects.

"Everything is beautifully curated, but nothing is precious," Ms. Kreamer said.

"And Stephen is boundlessly curious and interested in people. Or maybe he's just a frustrated bed-and-breakfast owner."

Mr. Chao is without a doubt preternaturally gregarious and energetic. He collects people the way others accrue vintage furniture, though he does that, too, particularly early-20th-century office furniture

The houses were built with two apartments: a studio and a one-bedroom. Mr. Chao opened each bungalow into a single dwelling for friends and family.

and vintage surfboards.

Patiently batting away his interruptions during a reporter's visit, Ms. Mansur said, "Stephen will talk to just about anyone." She recalled how he began quizzing Floriana Gavriel, a German designer sitting near them at a concert of the British indie band the xx. A month or so later, Ms. Gavriel and

Mr. Chao renovated the kitchen in one of the units, so his mother, a retired English professor and a serious cook, and his stepfather could use it.

her boyfriend moved into Unit G for a week, and she and Ms. Mansur began to plan a leather goods company, their collaboration a testament to the incubating properties of the Chao Pound. Ms. Gavriel spent six weeks in Unit H, after which their label, Mansur Gavriel, opened for business.

As for Ms. Mansur, she came to the compound through a friendship (platonic) with Mr. Chao's adopted brother, Thomas Ma, who was camping in Unit H while he worked at WonderHowTo, an instructional video site and Mr. Chao's latest company. Mr. Ma introduced Ms. Mansur to Chinese cooking and their mother, Phebe Chao, a retired Bennington English professor.

Mrs. Chao is also a serious cook, and she took a shine to Ms. Mansur, broadening her culinary education with dishes like ginger shrimp and the Chao family specialty, Chinese spaghetti: spaghetti with ground pork, bamboo and bell peppers. Ms. Mansur said she had already fallen in love with the Chao family when she invited Mr. Chao to a concert by Andrew W. K. (of "Party Til You Puke" fame) five years ago.

Mr. Chao may have fallen in love with Ms. Mansur a bit earlier. On a trip to Tijuana with Mr. Ma and Ms. Mansur, he bought "this horribly ugly object," he said, describing a plywood key caddy printed with a photo of woman's behind, promoting the Mexican soccer team. "It was just terrible. My intention was to offend everybody, but Rachel thought it was funny and kept it."

Since then, the two have embarked on numerous field trips, including an expedition to Liberia with the magician David Blaine to hunt down a guy named Winston who practices an arcane body trick called water spouting. Clearly, Ms. Mansur is an extremely good sport.

In 2000, Mr. Chao was a divorced father of two young sons, Madison and Virgil, when he bought the property for $2 million. "I thought we'd keep all the doors open, put in a dirt track and a half-pipe, and call it a day," he said, imagining each bungalow as a separate "room" and function: one for eating, one for sleeping, and so on. The six

bungalows had been built as 12 apartments, each with a studio and a one-bedroom. Local lore says that Louis B. Mayer used to stash his writers there, Mr. Chao said, "and tell them, 'Don't leave until you're finished.' Although there's no proof that's true."

At the time, the courtyard formed by the houses was open to the street, and Mr. Chao quickly realized that his neighbors were in the habit of treating the place like a public park. There were regulars: the homeless woman who liked to sleep in Unit J; the couple who picked the flowers; the woman who walked her dog there and said tartly, when Mr. Chao asked her not to: "I know someone here. Why don't you go

ABOVE: At the back of the compound is a barn that Mr. Chao uses as his office and work shed. RIGHT: The dining table in the main house can seat 18; Mr. Chao bought it from a consignment store. The banker's chairs were collected one at a time at flea markets and the Brimfield Antique Show.

back to the country you came from?"

It took some years for him to persuade the City of Santa Monica to approve his renovations, which included connecting the street-front bungalows (and closing off the courtyard) with a large room that now holds a Ping-Pong table. The property has been designated a landmark, and his plans were rejected numerous times.

Though there is no half-pipe, there are all sorts of child-friendly flourishes, like a loft bedroom for Virgil, his younger son, with a porthole overlooking the living room ("so when he had to go to bed, he could see what his brother was up to," Mr. Chao said) and which you can enter, or exit, with a rope.

And then there are the potato launchers, which Mr. Chao made with PVC pipe, and are an obsession he chased for years. You can see how to make one at WonderHowTo, an impish, addictive and exhaustive site that aggregates amateur video tutorials on a variety of subjects, from "soft mods" (how to make Siri pronounce your name correctly, for example) to cat pranks and how to redo the lettering on old appliances. Started in 2008 with Mike Goedecke, a filmmaker, it now has 10 million unique visitors each month, Mr. Chao said. Its catholic range is as good a biography of his appetites as anything.

After graduating from Harvard in 1977, Mr. Chao was given a fellowship to study the classics at Yale. He had packed up his VW bug when his mother phoned him. "Do you really want to spend the next six years of your life reading Greek and Latin?" he recalled her saying. "Since my mother is not the sort of parent to interfere, it stopped me cold."

It was early September, and the job postings board at Harvard "was like Dresden," he said. "There was nothing left except a farming job in Nantucket and one at The National Enquirer, which paid $36,000." So he took the latter.

It was a job ideally suited to Mr. Chao, even though he had no abiding interest in the marital problems of Farrah Fawcett and Lee Majors or incidences of alien abductions in Uruguay. He was happy, however, to chase these subjects down.

He went on to a career in television, creating "America's Most Wanted" for the Fox network. In 1992, he was three weeks into a four-year contract as president of Fox when he was fired for inviting a male stripper to perform at a company management retreat that Dick Cheney was attending — not as entertainment, he said, but to show that television networks were more prurient about nudity than violence.

Nonetheless, Rupert Murdoch paid out the lion's share of his salary, a gesture that unnerved Mr. Chao so much, he spent the next several weeks working at a local McDonald's. (A year later, he was hired back as a movie producer for Fox.)

"I was so disoriented," Mr. Chao said. "Not because I'd been fired, but because of the money. I had been making hit shows for Fox, but I hadn't been paid a lot. I was basically just a secretary when I created 'America's Most Wanted,' and all of sudden I got this really, really big check. I felt guilty for surviving."

Humbled by his time at McDonald's, the hardest job he has ever had, he said, he took up surfing. Since then, he has broken his nose and his eardrum, and nearly drowned when his board's leash became entangled in a coral reef in Cloudbreak, a famous swell in Fiji. The windows of the upstairs room in the barn, where he works, are papered with X-rays of his skull from the nose-breaking incident, because he thinks the patterns are curious and beautiful. (They are.)

The Chao Pound, he said, "is much more fun than owning a piece of art. It moves, it breathes and you can change it." Certainly it's tough enough to withstand Mr. Chao's enthusiasms. (As yet untried: a zip line from the top of the barn across the courtyard.)

He led a visitor into the barn's workroom to show off his collection of potato launchers. Ms. Mansur went to check the kitchen for ammunition, and came back empty-handed. Which is a good thing, because this reporter left with her hair unsinged and potato-free.

It took years for Mr. Chao to convince the city to allow him to close the compound to the street with this addition, a horizontal open room that neatly fits a Ping-Pong table.

WORTH THE WAIT

BY PENELOPE GREEN • PHOTOGRAPHS BY BRUCE BUCK

In New York City, successful real estate outcomes are largely a result of three qualities: patience, nerve and sheer luck. George Fares, a producer of television commercials, would seem to have all three.

In the early '90s, after moving from a 300-square-foot studio in Yorktown (rent: $265) to a one-bedroom on the Upper West Side (rent: $1,100), he began looking at townhouses. He thought, vaguely, that he would like to live in one someday and that, in any case, it would be a nice investment, particularly if he found a multi-family property.

It took five years before he made a bid, for this late-19th-century house in Chelsea — a bid he lost. Six months later, the house was for sale again, and he bought it for just over a million dollars.

The house had five apartments, but its details — moldings as intricate as the icing on a wedding cake, deliriously floral marble fireplaces, etched glass pocket doors — were intact.

His own apartment had gone condo, and he had met a young architect, Julian King, who had worked for Rafael Viñoly and Richard Meier and who practiced a kind of thoughtful, sensuous modernism that appealed to him. Mr. King made him a sleek bachelor pad featuring much white maple and concrete.

As the apartments in the townhouse became vacant, Mr. Fares asked Mr. King to spruce them up for the next tenant. Then the ground- and parlor-floor apartments became empty, and Mr. Fares moved in. He and Mr. King planned a renovation that scooped out the contemporary mistakes but left all the 19th-century details.

On the parlor floor, a small beige bedroom with painted-over window transoms became an airy, open kitchen and dining room. The original kitchen, a tiny cramped box on the ground floor, morphed into a master bathroom. A glass wall onto the garden is nearly invisible. Indeed, the "wall" is a sliding door that disappears, opening both the bedroom and the bathroom to the garden.

Everything was painted white; the rough, wide-planked pine floors were bleached; and the rooms were only minimally furnished, to give the details (those glorious moldings!) top billing.

There are all sorts of cunning flourishes. The master bath has one of those solid-stone sinks cantilevered out from the wall. But unlike many versions of this minimalist fantasy, where the pipes are hidden in a wall, and God help you when the inevitable leak or clog occurs, Mr. King tucked the pipes into a slim teak bench with a mitered access panel. And when you open the

The parlor floor of the late-19th-century townhouse has most of its original details, which were painted white. The rough pine floors were bleached and the rooms minimally furnished, to draw attention to the ornamentation.

medicine cabinet, you see the brick of the wall between this townhouse and the next, a satisfying archaeological reveal.

Mr. King also pushed the kitchen wall out 18 inches and hid all the ductwork inside it (a trick he learned while working for Mr. Meier on the Getty Center). The air now spills out from behind the luscious, floral molding, which was recreated by Architectural Sculpture and Restoration, a Brooklyn firm that specializes in ornamentation. Outside, the parlor-floor deck is connected to the garden by a steel-and-teak staircase, alongside of which a stucco wall masks more mechanicals. Topped with a planter of ornamental grasses, it's a spare, lovely volume.

The cost of the 2,500-square-foot project was about $200 a square foot, and it took two and a half years to complete, which was O.K. by Mr. Fares (see patience, above).

Mr. King, who has worked on the house now for nearly seven years, said: "I really got a chance to know the house. It's what I always tell clients, which is to live in a place for a year before you do anything, so you can see how the sun moves through it, and learn all its habits."

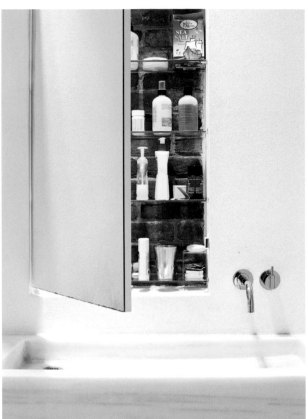

LICENSED TO GRILL

BY JULIE EARLE-LEVINE • PHOTOGRAPHS BY TREVOR TONDRO

Michael Diamond was sitting in his Cobble Hill town house, marveling at the virtues of a backyard. "When I was growing up in New York, we were the anomaly," said Mr. Diamond, better known as Mike D of the Beastie Boys. "Our family stayed, but back then families didn't stay. Once you had a second kid, you immediately left, so the kids could run around outside."

Mr. Diamond now has two boys of his own, Davis and Skyler, with his wife, Tamra Davis, a filmmaker. And the outdoor space is a recent addition. The family left their TriBeCa loft for what Mr. Diamond, who grew up on the Upper West Side, calls "the suburban dream in Brooklyn."

As his wife observed, there was a steep learning curve involved. "He had never lived outside of Manhattan," said Ms. Davis, who is from Southern California.

The result, however, was worth it. Now their older son can walk home from school by himself, an experience Mr. Diamond missed out on as a child, although his school was only two blocks away. "It was traumatic," he said. "A very different city."

Another advantage of life in Brooklyn: "We can have dinner outside," Mr. Diamond said, pointing out the basil they used in the previous night's pasta and the strawberry plants he hopes will grow. "The kids can eat, then run down and play basketball."

Renovating the 3,200-square-foot house wasn't nearly as challenging as moving to Brooklyn. That may be because he and Ms. Davis are so aesthetically compatible, Mr. Diamond said.

How would he describe their aesthetic?

"I think it's kind of vernacular, sensitive, modern," he said.

Ms. Davis interrupted: "Whoa."

"Does that sound pretentious?" he asked. "Well, I'm saying we are good at responding to prevailing culture in a house."

The renovation took about six months. "Our goal was to limit our total reno-architecture budget to under $500,000," he said. "Which we pretty much succeeded in. It meant that at times we'd splurge on one light fixture, but not another. And it helped because we ended up having to retain original detail, clean it up and leave it as is."

They moved the master bedroom to the top floor for privacy, ripping out the dropped ceiling to create a feeling of space and light. The adjoining bathroom is huge, with a tub in the center of the room.

The boys' rooms are on the floor below, "completely in their own world," Mr. Diamond said, with space in between for impromptu soccer games.

On the ground floor is a screening room

The chandelier is by Tord Boontje. When Tamra Davis needed a chandelier for the kitchen, she showed this one to her husband: "I said it was the most beautiful chandelier I have ever seen. He agreed."

Michael Diamond (better known as Mike D of the Beastie Boys), Tamra Davis and their two sons left a TriBeCa loft for a Brooklyn town house built around 1853. "We didn't completely tear out the kitchen for cost reasons," Ms. Davis said. "Just by changing the surface of the island and the counters" — which are now marble — "we had a whole new look."

and a home office that the couple share, in alternating shifts. Ms. Davis uses it when she is editing films; Mr. Diamond works on his own projects here and at Oscilloscope Laboratories, the independent film company co-founded by Adam Yauch, the Beastie Boys member who died last year. "It has to be for a couple of months each," Mr. Diamond said. "Dual-use concurrently doesn't work."

Most of all, the house has given them peace and privacy. "Lofts are great," Mr. Diamond said. "But with a home, there is a lot to be said for delineated space. To have the luxury of a little separate work space is huge — and to have the dream-sequence master bath."

Apart from adding a marble island and a backsplash for the stove, they didn't do much to the kitchen, which is mostly Ms. Davis's domain. She is the one with the online cooking show, after all, and the vegetarian cookbook to her name.

But Mr. Diamond takes exception to the suggestion that he doesn't cook, and is quick to note that he's considering buying a barbecue for grilling fish and vegetables on the deck. "For a dude, I think I do cook," he said. "I'm a stay-at-home parent a lot of the time."

He paused and considered.

"What is the right term for that?" he said. "I'm a multi-dad."

The master bathroom is one of the couple's favorite places in the house. "We had to reinforce the floors to hold the heavy tub and two people," Ms. Davis said. In the master bedroom, they knocked out the ceiling and were surprised at the height; the beams are original.

BACK IN THE ('30S) U.S.S.R.

BY ANDREW E. KRAMER • PHOTOGRAPHS BY ANDREA WYNER

Midway through the restoration of a stately old top-floor apartment in one of this city's fashionable neighborhoods, the owner swiveled to adopt an entirely new plan. It was more than a shift in the color scheme.

"I decided I wanted to design the apartment in the style of a senior bureaucrat of the early Stalin period," said the owner, Sergei Bobovnikov. And so began a renovation that was unusual even by Russian standards.

Sleek and flashy is common here today. A meditation on the country's design history, with its leftist language of agricultural and working-class decorative elements, is less common, but not unheard-of.

Even so, the space in question was hardly evocative of Politburo luxury when Mr. Bobovnikov bought it in 2002. Originally designed as a single residence, it had become a decrepit communal space occupied by eight families in a row of small rooms along a lightless corridor.

Mr. Bobovnikov, who had recently divorced and needed a new home, intended to refurbish it in a modern, comfortable style. But the history of the early 20th-century building, which had been home to a number of influential Stalinist-era officials and served as a backdrop for the Great Purge of the late 1930s, seemed to call for some kind of commentary, he thought: a grander, more artistic statement that would not attempt to conceal this defining moment in the country's history.

The idea of creating a Stalinist-era interior gradually took shape as he knocked down the walls that divided the apartment into small, dark rooms, revealing its original generous proportions, a hallmark of 1930s Russian Art Deco. It was, to be sure, not entirely a bolt from the blue. Mr. Bobovnikov is an antiques dealer specializing in the ideological art of the early Soviet period.

"The concept was clearly forming in my mind," he said. "I had a lot of items I really liked but hadn't sold, and they fit here like a mosaic."

He is quick to clarify that he is no Stalin sympathizer. "Stalinism is repulsive, like Fascism," said Mr. Bobovnikov, who decided to use the apartment as a place to show off his art and meet with clients, as well as a space for overnight guests, instead of as his primary residence. "But Italian Fascist design, for example, is very popular now, and I understand why, as I like it myself. I didn't know when I started that Stalinism would be a trend, too."

As it happens, Stalin Empire style, which draws on Art Deco and the clean lines of Mussolini-era Italian design, is enjoying something of a mini-revival in Russia, said

Visitors are greeted by a Lenin rug in the entry hall. Rugs like this were made in the 1960s and 1970s and intended to be hung on the wall.

Xenia Adjoubei, a lecturer in architectural history and theory at the British Higher School of Art and Design who also has a design practice in Moscow.

Stalinist-era interiors are now widely appreciated for their beautiful and minimalist look, she said. But recreating one of those interiors from scratch, she acknowledged, might strike some as odd, even a little creepy.

"But it is only unnerving if you see this person as wanting to recreate the lifestyle of a member of the NKVD," Ms. Adjoubei said, referring to the secret police of the 1930s. "He's probably just appreciating the aesthetic value."

Mr. Bobovnikov's interest in the style, however, wasn't purely aesthetic: He wanted to provoke conversations about this episode in the country's history with anyone who visited, he said, by highlighting the contrast of the exuberance and optimism of the art and decorative accessories with "the understanding of how it all ended for these people." So he decorated the apartment to look as if it belonged to a member of the 1930s Leningrad Soviet, or city council, with baubles and art to match.

Various Stalin-era officials did, in fact, call this building home, if not for long. One was Sergei Kirov, the prominent Bolshevik leader whose 1934 assassination marked the beginning of Stalin's Great Purge, in which more than a million people were imprisoned or executed. Many other residents died during another wave of mass arrests known as the Leningrad Case of 1949.

But even in a building with such a dramatic history, achieving the look of that period was not easy more than a half-century later. Mr. Bobovnikov spent four years and the equivalent of about $75,000 renovating the apartment, not including the cost of the antiques and art, some of which are now built into the property.

Creating the appropriate atmosphere, he discovered, was all in the details. One closet, for example, is made from tractor-themed bas-relief oak paneling that was originally in the library of the direc-

RIGHT: The rug in the children's room is from Ikea; the porcelain fireplace is non-working. This room was purposely "not burdened with ideology," Sergei Bobovnikov said. TOP: Mr. Bobovnikov with his Chrysler PT Cruiser.

Ул. Жореса

19 ☆ 27
Береги
уголь i дрова

The idea of creating a Stalinist-era interior took shape as the walls that divided the apartment into small, dark rooms were knocked down, revealing its original generous proportions, a hallmark of 1930s Russian Art Deco.

ABOVE: A Lenin paperweight sits beside a custom-made tile.
RIGHT: The fireplace is decorated with a bronze bas-relief of Stalin.

tor of the Kirov Tractor Factory. Another rare and valuable ensemble, an oak chair and desk set, has a "Bread of Communism" agricultural theme carved by one of the designers of the Order of Lenin lapel pin. And period Socialist Realist paintings adorn the walls, among them an eerie depiction of a group of schoolchildren admiring a statue of Joseph Stalin.

Other design details are modern riffs on Soviet themes. In the kitchen, a new Italian stove is festooned with period design elements, including a stamped bronze sheet from the cafeteria of a Soviet electrical utility that depicts a hammer and sickle pierced by a lightning bolt; the handle on the oven door is a samovar spigot.

The bathroom is done in the style of a shower room at a Soviet sports hall; industrial lights from a tugboat were repurposed to illuminate the mirror.

The apartment's long hallway is tiled in the style of a Soviet-era institution, in a bone-and-green color scheme that is no longer available; Mr. Bobovnikov had the tiles custom-made.

He said he gets several calls a week from interior designers asking how to replicate various aspects of the interior. And as for his antiques clients? Most of them are older businessmen or government employees, he said, who were raised on Soviet movies depicting similar settings for the elite and powerful of an earlier generation. Seeing one of those interiors brought to life, he said, they become almost giddy. "People like the atmosphere," he said.

"They wouldn't like to live here," he added, "but they like to visit."

The bathroom is done in the style of a shower room at a Soviet sports hall. The handles on the shower doors are submarine valves, found at a Moscow flea market, and the sign on the ceiling reads "washroom."

207

SCRAPING AWAY THE DECADES

BY TIM MCKEOUGH • PHOTOGRAPHS BY JANE BEILES

The restoration began with a valiant swing of the sledgehammer. Robert Highsmith and Stefanie Brechbuehler knew that somewhere inside the house they had bought was a quaint 1850s structure, but the 20th-century additions made it almost impossible to see.

"There was this terrible little porch on the front held up by two little sticks that looked like someone just bought it at Home Depot," said Mr. Highsmith. "I thought, I don't care what this does to the house, I'm ripping it off. At some point, you just have to take the plunge."

And so began nine months of hard labor. The couple, who are partners in the up-and-coming Brooklyn design firm Workstead, spent their weekends peeling, scraping and sanding away undesirable features like asbestos shingle siding and linoleum flooring, revealing original details like clapboard siding and wide-plank pine floors with square-head nails.

"It felt like undressing something," said Ms. Brechbuehler. "There was this beautiful thing underneath and we just had to remove the layers to get to it."

The couple found the house shortly after they were married nearby in the summer of 2011. After falling for Columbia County's rolling hills and winding country roads, they dreamed about what it would be like to own a house there.

Before that, Mr. Highsmith said, "we were the kind of people who didn't realize you could drive out of the city and get somewhere totally different." Living in New York, he added, "you get into this mindset of flying to the other side of the country to get away."

They bought the property that fall and began planning their renovation for the spring. But as a young couple with a growing business, they couldn't afford the kind of full-blown renovation they would have done for their clients. Instead, they did most of the work themselves, with help from handy parents and a neighbor who is a contractor. As Ms. Brechbuehler said, "It was a whole lot of sweat equity."

After entertaining ambitious plans that involved changing everything, Mr. Highsmith said, "We brought it back down to earth and decided to just strip it down and make it simple and beautiful."

"Painting everything white is the oldest trick in the book," Robert Highsmith said. "And there's a reason why" — it makes rooms feel light and airy.

Robert Highsmith
and Stefanie
Brechbuehler,
partners in the
Brooklyn design firm
Workstead, knew that
their home dated to
the 1850s, although
later additions
made it hard to see.
So they decided
to "strip it down
and make it simple
and beautiful," Mr.
Highsmith said.

RIGHT: The couple cut down a $300 four-poster bed to fit their low-ceilinged bedroom. The wall lamp is a vintage George Kovacs model. BELOW: The beds in the guest bedroom belonged to Mr. Highsmith's grandparents.

Still, that required installing new drywall on the upstairs ceiling, replacing missing windows, tracking down and customizing an antique front door that fit the character of the house and painting expanses of dark interior paneling white. One day, after working straight through the daylight hours, they decided to paint a closet at 2 a.m. because they were so thrilled with the transformation.

"Painting everything white is the oldest trick in the book," Mr. Highsmith said. "And there's a reason why" — it immediately refreshes rooms and makes them feel light and airy.

Capping the renovation cost at around $30,000, they kept the existing mustard-colored oven and the laminate countertops in the kitchen, updating the cabinets with more white paint and big wooden knobs.

Then they furnished the two-bedroom home with a mix of inexpensive antique finds, family heirlooms and inventive pieces they customized themselves. Friends are always impressed with the corner sofa in the living room, Ms. Brechbuehler said. It's from Ikea, but sits on turned wooden legs the couple found at Lowe's. Mr. Highsmith performed a more extreme transformation of an old army cot, turning it into a coffee table by replacing the canvas sling with a wooden top. And the objet d'art in the corner of the living room is a crushed metal bucket that he recovered from a pile of trash at the bottom of the hill behind their house.

The Shaker-inspired interior has inspired the couple to lead simpler lives when they're in the house, Ms. Brechbuehler said: "We decided to have technology-free weekends." Sometimes, she added, "we turn everything off, and don't use iPads, iPhones, or watch movies."

It has the unexpected effect of extending the weekend, Mr. Highsmith said. "You realize how long your day can be," he said, "when you're not occupying yourself with checking e-mail."

LIVING IN SEPIA

BY PENELOPE GREEN • PHOTOGRAPHS BY RANDY HARRIS

They were the dandies of Avenue C, swanning about in cutaway suit coats, top hats and detachable starched collars. They made paintings the old-fashioned way, dressed in smocks and using rabbit skin glue primer and lead gesso on linen tacked, rather than stapled, to stretchers they found in the garbage. They backdated their work to the early 1900s, or before.

At a time when appropriation was one of the many art strategies of the moment, David McDermott and Peter McGough took that practice (among others) to its extreme. "Time maps," they called their work, which tackled themes like sexuality, bigotry and the AIDS crisis.

Even their habitats were in the past tense, with 19th-century furniture and wallpaper, illuminated by candles and often without heat or plumbing. (Mr. McDermott, the more dogmatic of the two, had a habit of ripping out all the modern appliances, even if the apartment was a rental, to the extreme dismay of many a landlord.) But as specific as their lifestyle was, Mr. McDermott and Mr. McGough fit right into their neighborhood, the polymorphous cultural soup that was the East Village art scene in the early 1980s.

Glenn O'Brien cast Mr. McGough as an extra in his New Wave movie, "Downtown 81," with Jean-Michel Basquiat. Fab Five Freddy was a friend. They worked in studios discarded by Julian Schnabel. They fought over an apartment with Kenny Scharf and Keith Haring. Their work was collected in the 1987 Whitney Biennial.

Nearly three decades later, Mr. McDermott and Mr. McGough — otherwise known as McDermott & McGough, to give them their art world tag — are still collaborating and performing, which is another way of describing their period-perfect lifestyle, although they are now on opposite sides of the Atlantic. They've racked up two more Biennials. They have moved from painting to photography and film, and back again. Their show "Suspicious of Rooms Without Music or Atmosphere," a series of paintings of scenes from old movies in which the actress is caught in a moment of extreme emotion, biting her knuckles, eyes welling with tears or wide with fear, is an appropriate manifesto for what is still the two men's worldview.

Mr. McDermott has been living in Ireland since the 1990s (initially in a highly atmospheric house in Dublin made even more so by his removal of its kitchen appliances). But Mr. McGough is here in New York, in a one-bedroom apartment in a 1930s rental building in the West Village. He has fitted it out with 1930s furniture — "in the Continental style," as he put it — much of it Italian Moderne and taken from a house in Milan. There's a foot-high vintage radio,

Peter McGough, half of the time-bending art duo McDermott & McGough, has traded in the 19th century for a life of modernity, circa 1930, in an apartment of that period in the West Village. The painting by them on the wall, "What Will I Tell My Heart?," shows Virna Lisi at top and Anne Francis at bottom.

FOLLOWING SPREAD: The sofa was designed by Daniel Romualdez with fabric from Jed Johnson Home. "I spent a lot on this apartment," Mr. McGough said. "It's expensive to live in the past."

two telephones from the 1930s and a cubist lamp with an elaborate handmade shade. The light switches have been replaced with vintage plates; the contemporary kitchen is hidden by a curtain.

"Of course, McDermott wanted me to rip it out," Mr. McGough said of his kitchen. "It's my first grown-up apartment in a long time. I spent a lot of money decorating it" — easily $75,000, he estimated. "It's expensive to live in the past."

And yet, a 1930s building? That's awfully modern, given the appetites of Messrs. McDermott and McGough. Has Mr. McGough lapsed?

"I didn't lapse," he told a visitor. "I just moved to a different period."

On that morning, Mr. McGough was reflecting on a life in houses, which also happens to be a story of lost houses.

"And we lost a lot of houses," he said. "I think of that line from 'The Maltese Falcon': 'This is the stuff dreams are made of.' That's what we do. We were never just old-timey twee queens sitting with teacups, although we were doing that, too. With McDermott, you had to enter the past, you had to walk into another dimension. When he was a teenager, he made a conscious decision not to live in the present. For him, it wasn't decorating, it was an installation and an immersion. Who's to say, if you were sitting in our 18th-century house, on our furniture, that you hadn't been transported to the 18th century?"

If Mr. McDermott is, as Mr. O'Brien said, the theorist, "the true believer," Mr. McGough is the curator of that vision, the one who turned the dogma into an object, like a painting or a cyanotype photograph. "And while it may have seemed like a kind of camp," Mr. O'Brien said, recalling "the circus" of Mr. McDermott and Mr. McGough's old-world accouterments, which by the late 1980s included a Model T Ford and a horse-drawn carriage, "it was always rooted in something more sound," if you concede that a style or what seems merely decorative can actually be political.

There was a moment when the duo set themselves up as actual decorators, Mr.

McGough said, but "it went south fast." They had been thrown out of an apartment in Hudson, N.Y., because the building was being condemned, and had moved into one on Avenue A and Houston. They called themselves Knickerbocker Decorative Arts Inc., and they had two clients, one a businessman with a studio apartment.

"It did not go well," Mr. McGough said. "McDermott took out all the electricity. There couldn't be a plastic bag. The food in the cupboards had to be just right. It was really an installation, and for McDermott, it had to be perfect. He has a pretty short fuse. There was no room for a television, so we went back to painting pretty quickly."

Before the money came in, they would beg meals at friends' apartments, dropping in for coffee and toast, and moving on if they weren't offered any. They were resolute in their decision not to work, Mr. McGough said. "If we did, that meant we weren't artists. We'd go two days without eating. We were skeletons with good hair." And slim enough to fit in the detachable collars they favored, he added.

After their first real show, they moved into the top floor of a house on Avenue C, where Mr. McDermott ripped out all the appliances, enraging their landlord. " 'You've ruined my property,' " Mr. McGough recalled him saying. "McDermott told him,

The front hall is papered in a reproduction of a 1930s vintage print. Mr. McGough's friend Fernando Santangelo helped him find the wallpaper and choose the apartment's colors.

PREVIOUS SPREAD: The Brazilian mahogany bed set is Italian Moderne. The blankets are from the 1920s.

'No, we're improving it.' "

They turned an old bank building in Williamsburg, Brooklyn, into their studio and walked to work over the Williamsburg Bridge with a dogcart, an old wagon harnessed to their two springer spaniels, and their two terrified dachshunds inside. At the suggestion of a curator, Diego Cortez, and their gallerist, Howard Read, they began photographing their life using a 1915 camera they found at a flea market.

As their fortunes improved, they bought a 1790s "miniature mansion" on nine acres in the Catskills and kitted it out in period style. There was an outhouse in back, a paddock for their horses and an old general store next door that they also purchased. It took six hours, Mr. McGough said, to get there in their Model T, driving the back roads in their top hats. There was so much money in the art world in the 1980s, and they were awash in it. "We thought it was like an endless lemonade fountain," Mr. McGough said. "We thought it would never end. We had never had money before, and we never saved a dime. It was an odd period. There was all this money, and you're in your 20s, and all your friends are dying."

When they were unable to pay their taxes, they lost their house in the Catskills and all its contents, along with their vintage cars, their carriages and their horses in a three-day auction in Albany. And when their landlord on Avenue C sold the townhouse, they were thrown out of there, too, and Mr. McDermott moved to Ireland. Mr. McGough shipped him the contents of the Avenue C house, and together they made another environment in Dublin, though Mr. McGough moved back to New York City after five years. (Eventually, the landlord of the Dublin house died, and Mr. McDermott was evicted; he is now camping in his studio there.)

"We were showing in Europe and having this European life, but Dublin was an odd place to be in your 30s," Mr. McGough said. "I wasn't young, I was an outsider. I didn't enjoy drinking. And it rained all the time."

By contrast, Mr. McDermott, he said, had had his heart broken by the United

States and was committed to his new country. He took Irish citizenry around 2005.

At that point, Mr. McGough was living in a fifth-floor walk-up on East 46th Street and chafing at the constraints of their work. "I realized I didn't want to do another detachable collar painting, or another pretty boy," he said. "I wanted to change the time frame. I went back to my childhood, when I would watch old movies obsessively."

What those movies promised, he said, was an escape from the banality and the prison of suburbia. The paintings McDermott and McGough are making now are all about an actress's cinematic moment.

Above a hand-blown fish bowl from the 1830s, a portrait of Mr. McGough by Anh Duong; spectator shoes for summer.

"Will she kill the husband, or walk out on him?" Mr. McGough said. "I think of all the decisions I've made, bad and good, and where they have taken me."

The rejiggering of the career, he said, was a wake-up call. "It's been successful, and it made me decide I'm going to get a real apartment and not live in a studio. I went mad to decorate. Look at this wallpaper," he said, pointing to the print in the front hall. "We love wallpaper. McDermott says wallpaper changes one's life."

He and Mr. McDermott talk daily. No longer romantically involved, they remain connected. "We have collaborated on our life and art since 1980," he said. "The ideas

for both come from both of us. And if a painting is made in our Bushwick studio, or David puts his patched long underwear on an old hanger in a show in Ireland, it's always McDermott & McGough."

He added: "I think beauty on its own is enough. People always told us we lived in a fantasy, in a bubble, but the world is a very harsh place."

As for all the objects he has surrounded himself with — the tickets, as he might say, for a bit of time travel — "when I die, they'll have no meaning. Who knows how long I have? But boy, have I had a great life. All the failures and all the successes. And I drove to Canada in a Model T."

The Fiestaware china belonged to Mr. McDermott's grandmother. The painting of Mr. McDermott, at left, is by Edward Brezinski; the drawing of Mr. McGough, right, is by Mr. McDermott. The curtain at left hides the contemporary kitchen.

227

MARRIAGE IS YARD WORK

BY MICHAEL TORTORELLO • PHOTOGRAPHS BY LAURE JOLIET

One Thursday evening, the United States Navy notified Ryan Benoit that instead of tracking the $150 million overhaul of the Essex, an 844-foot-long air and amphibious assault ship, he should probably drink a couple of gin and tonics with his wife and water the drooping lettuce in his planter. This being the year of the Great Congressional Sequester, the next day was Furlough Friday. And Mr. Benoit, a civilian port engineer and a lieutenant commander in the Navy Reserve, would be spending the accidental holiday in the garden.

"I'm being told not to answer the phone," Mr. Benoit said. This slackness was a shock to his routine. "I'm always doing something. I very rarely get to relax."

Orders are orders. But there was work to be done at home, too: a renovation of the yard that was almost as ambitious as the warship's and only a little less reliant on industrial supplies. For the last four years, Mr. Benoit and his wife, Chantal Aida Gordon, have been creating the quintessential outdoor room, a couple of blocks from the surfers' paradise known as Windansea Beach in this city's La Jolla section.

The house? A two-bedroom, one-bath rental. A little over 750 square feet. Speak of it no more.

As for the yard? This will be a place to host dinner parties and screen Chargers games and stash a shortboard and shower off and plant cactuses and harvest guava and blend cocktails and sleep off a hangover and catch up on back issues of *The New Yorker*. You know, that kind of space.

It will also be a place to blog. As of this spring, the design project has turned into a new garden-and-style site, TheHorticult.com. The yard is now a backdrop for photographing D.I.Y. delphinium garlands and Wellington boots by Le Chameau.

It's a lot to ask of a 55-by-44-foot, concrete-covered lot. And to the extent that the couple is building practically every piece of furniture and planting every container, it's a lot to ask of themselves. You might say that Ms. Gordon and Mr. Benoit are not transforming the garden so much as the garden is transforming them.

Julian Mackler, a longtime friend who photographed the couple's wedding, has watched this change take root. "Some people want to stay on the sidelines, and some people want to get their hands dirty," he said on the phone from Harlem. "I never see people my age take such care of a garden unless they're a straight-up hippie."

Ms. Gordon moved from New York University to an editorial-assistant post in the West Coast office of *Vogue*. (You can see her introducing Lauren Conrad to the copy

The yard, a concrete-covered lot transformed into the quintessential outdoor room, is a place to host dinner parties, plant cactuses, harvest guava, blend cocktails and sleep off a hangover.

machine in the first few episodes of MTV's docudrama "The Hills.") Mr. Benoit attended the United States Merchant Marine Academy, in Kings Point, N.Y. And for a couple of East Coast transplants, the quest for a classic Southern California space has inspired a shift in consciousness.

"At work, I'm in an industrial environment: no plants, no nothing, just a steel structure," Mr. Benoit said. "It's the opposite of when I come home."

Ms. Gordon looked at her husband sympathetically. "Don't you think some of those old guys grow some tomatoes?"

The blog has revealed the earthy proclivities of many of their urbane friends. "I couldn't believe the number of people who got excited about the jacaranda story," she said, referring to a post about the omnipresent San Diego trees that bloom purple in late May. "Ten years ago, I wouldn't have been able to spot a jacaranda."

Mr. Benoit said, "Four months ago, I wouldn't have been able to recognize a jacaranda."

Ms. Gordon added, "It just deepens your experience when you're walking down the street and you know what a tree is."

Before Ms. Gordon was a gardener, she was a writer. She volunteered at a community garden in East Harlem to research a coming-of-age novel, titled "The Fame and Exile of the Lotus Eaters." It chronicles the escapades of a "teenage nerd" who discovers a new lotus cultivar.

"The flower becomes an overnight hit in Manhattan, the way those things do," she said. "Things go downhill when her friends start using the flower as a study drug." (As a day job, she works anonymously as a copywriter for a business strategist.)

Before Mr. Benoit was a gardener, he was a photographer. On his travels as a reservist, or with Ms. Gordon, he would fill up memory cards with botanical photos. Not infrequently, he has coaxed his wife into these pictures. In botanical terms, Ms. Gordon would classify as willowy, with rufous hair and a slightly maculate complexion. Put plainly, she has the kind of

looks that might stand out in a nightclub, which happens to be where the couple met.

"You're easy to photograph, babe," he said.

"Thanks, babe," she said.

The house the pair moved into as newlyweds six years ago was virgin ground. That's probably too generous a description. As their friend and across-the-street neighbor, David Deitch, said, "That house, before they moved in, was a shambles."

Ms. Gordon recalled, "Our neighbor's ficus was growing into the yard."

Mr. Benoit added, "There wasn't much here to work with."

Whatever the couple's aesthetic was at that point, it wasn't the shaggy look. They discovered an expression of their nascent style on weekend trips to Palm Springs, Calif., where they basked in spots like the Ace Hotel (rehabbed by the Los Angeles design firm Commune) and the Parker Palm Springs (by Jonathan Adler). Every room and patio seemed to showcase a different material. Ceramics and tiles butted up against leather ottomans and Navajo rugs. Ms. Gordon described the style as "a riot of different patterns and colors. You don't think it will work, but it makes a lot of emotional sense."

She and Mr. Benoit began to reimagine their midcentury ranch house here as it might have appeared in a 1960s photo spread from *Sunset* magazine. Mr. Benoit fell under the design influence of Southern California philosopher kings like Richard Neutra and Rudolph Schindler.

"We liked the idea of being able to step outside and just have it be another living space," he said. Alas, there was no seamless glass membrane. "If we owned a place ourselves, it would be nice to be able to open the space."

Ms. Benoit said, "So you can see straight out of the other side to the pool."

Of course, there was no pool, either. And however much the couple appreciated the vintage furnishings in the boutiques of Palm Springs, Mr. Benoit said, "We couldn't afford any of that stuff."

The furnishings the couple could afford, Mr. Benoit recalled, were junk. Specifically, industrial surplus from a warehouse near

"I like garden design that's a little bit more heavy and masculine, in general," said Ryan Benoit, who was a photographer before he was a gardener. On his travels as a reservist, or with his wife, Chantal Aida Gordon, he would fill up memory cards with botanical photos.

the shipyards where, he said, "they sell stuff for just above scrap." This is how they ended up with a planter made out of a ship's horn, the size and shape of a sousaphone.

Or take the outdoor bar table where Mr. Benoit was sitting. "I call this a rolling entertainment arbor," he said. Over the course of a day, you could make coffee on the 41-inch-high Douglas fir tabletop, transplant a few succulents and then plug in the laptop. And it was an ideal spot for a light dinner.

At that prompt, Ms. Gordon disappeared gracefully to put together a plate of ceviche and chips, takeout from Oscar's Mexican Seafood down the road.

"Do you want any cava, babe?" she asked.

"Yeah, babe," he said.

The frame for the piece came from two industrial stepladders. "I think I bought them for a total of $60," he said. And the whole battlewagon rolls on eight beefy industrial casters.

Mr. Benoit rose from his stool, as if to give it a spin. Then he grabbed on to the rafters overhead and pulled himself halfway through a chin-up. "I like garden design that's a little bit more heavy and masculine, in general," he said. (He has started to post prototypes on a separate site, Ryan Benoit Design.)

A feminine balance, he said, came from the plants the couple liked to install in his furniture. This is mostly Ms. Gordon's portfolio, and she wandered over to what they call the "living table," a coffee table fitted together out of $50 worth of Douglas fir two-by-sixes. A cruciform shape at the

TOP, FROM LEFT: The coffee table, planted with succulents; wall containers made from ammo cans; corner seating; a modular table.

BOTTOM: Routine maintenance; the garden kitchen; a mobile side table Mr. Benoit built; an area devoted to carnivorous plants.

center makes an inset planting bed, rather like a sunken living room for '70s swingers.

Ms. Gordon knelt down to pet a few favorite specimens. The Lithops marmorata, a clumping succulent, resembled an upside-down unicorn's hoof. Far-fetched, perhaps, but then Ms. Gordon's favorite plants often possess a quality of fantasy. It's no accident, perhaps, that one of her most popular springtime blog posts cataloged the botany of the Seven Kingdoms on "Game of Thrones."

Desert plants are nothing if not permutations on the improbable. "It's like buying a little living sculpture," she said.

By contrast, the couple is happy to leave the food gardening to the professionals, Mr. Benoit said. "To be honest with you, we don't grow vegetables, because I don't really like the way they look."

He pointed to a silver-colored form nestled beneath the woolly rose (Echeveria Doris Taylor). The common name for this species was galvanized pipe, and the black shoot under the cap was an HDMI cable. To be clear, this was not a plant but the hookup to the outdoor projector for the "hideaway theater."

The screen is camouflaged, too. Mr. Benoit circled a neatly trimmed rosemary shrub and stopped at a trellis frame in the shape of a window. Reaching behind the fascia beam at the top, he pulled down a 91-inch-diagonal screen.

The rosemary released a puff of perfume where he had brushed against it. Sitting on the chaise longue, made out of wood salvaged from Ms. Gordon's old futon, you could see the foliage shadowing the bottom inch of the screen like a movie curtain.

Mr. Benoit has also found a way to backlight the hedge, with a strip of LEDs. "I call it garden stadium lighting," he said. "There's not a lot of stylish lighting options out there. I learned to solder to do these."

He added, "I love bringing technology to the garden, too."

The Horticult blog has shaped up to be something of an I.T. project as well. The beauty shots on the right rail of the front page fall under the heading "Plants We're Loving on Instagram." And for many species mentioned on the blog, the couple harvests hashtags to aggregate in Instagram galleries. Search the term #octopusagave, for instance, and The Horticult rakes up a scrapbook of undulating leaves.

They call this page the Community Garden. But the phrase is somewhat aspirational. There isn't a lot of personal horticulture going on in the community itself. Dr. Deitch, a professor emeritus of psychiatry at the University of California, San Diego, who has lived on the block for more than 20 years, guessed that only two or three families maintain their own yards. In La Jolla, as in so many other fashionable neighborhoods, gardening is something you pay someone else to do.

"Ideally, we'd like to be able to own this place," Mr. Benoit said.

Ms. Gordon said, "We go to open houses."

Their friends wonder aloud, "Why are you doing all this to a yard that isn't yours?" Mr. Benoit said. "In truth, 90 percent of this stuff is coming with us."

The built-ins could be termed built-outs. Almost all the furniture is modular or sits on wheels. Everything moves: the Preway fireplace (Craigslist, $300), the outdoor kitchen with the sink and cabinets, even the deck. "Most of this stuff I can have in the driveway in three hours," he said.

Ms. Gordon served homemade cantaloupe ice pops, with garden mint that grows in their ammo-can herb planters. The garden lights were glowing, and bossa nova was humming from the outdoor speakers. Mr. Benoit was drinking Riesling now. And the "babes" rolled off the tongue with a Parisian lilt, bébé.

The couple has designed the yard for entertaining, sure. But at a certain point in the evening, it seemingly becomes something else: the couple's private nightclub.

It was 1 a.m. when Mr. Benoit finally rose from the picnic table and wandered off to someplace totally unexpected. For the first time in six hours, he stepped inside the house.

The yard is designed for entertaining. But at a certain point in the evening, it seemingly becomes something else: the couple's private nightclub.

NOTHING FANCY

BY JESS CHAMBERLAIN • PHOTOGRAPHS BY JEREMY BITTERMANN

If Brian and Jill Faherty's home looks a little like a catalog, there's a good reason: Mr. Faherty is the owner of Schoolhouse Electric & Supply Co., the lighting and housewares company based in Portland, Ore., and his ranch-style house here is where most of the catalogs are shot.

But it's also where he tests products in development, and where he and his wife are raising three children (J. P., Greta, and Audrey). So while it may look as if everything is arranged just so, in fact the opposite is true. Things are constantly in flux, and function is more important than appearance.

The main piece of furniture in the family room, for instance, is an Ikea sofa. "We added brass-walnut accented legs for a sleeker look," said Mr. Faherty. "We like to invest in some things for enduring quality, but a sectional couch with three kids — how long is that going to last before it has to be reupholstered?"

He added: "We don't want to be worried about our couch. We live here."

Even the house was chosen for its utility, and for the ways in which it differed from their previous home, a Colonial-style house with great bones but very small rooms. As Mrs. Faherty, a product developer for Schoolhouse Electric, said: "We had a 4,700-square-foot house, but we'd end up in the 150-square-foot TV room to be together."

Like many of the couple's products, their 3,200-square-foot house has a midcentury foundation, but the design has been reimagined for modern life. In this case, that involved reconfiguring the layout of the 1958 house, which they bought in 2012, but retaining its footprint and the three brick fireplaces.

Ben Waechter, a local architect, created a family-friendly floor plan for them, with wide hallways, large windows and a central living space that combined the dining room, kitchen, home office and family room.

"They wanted a single-story house made of forms and materials that would transcend any idea of time or style," Mr. Waechter said. "Images of Swedish courtyard farmhouses came to mind." The renovation, which was completed in only five months, cost about $500,000.

Although (or perhaps because) the new house has less space, Mr. Faherty said, it functions better than the large house they gave up. "We live in every square inch of this house," he said. "There's no wasted space at all."

And considering that "it's going by so fast with our kids," he said, what's even better is that "it's like the family lodge here: We get to see so much more of them."

With all that open space and an outdoor

A Schoolhouse Electric chandelier hangs over a table made by Brian Faherty, Keith Schrader and Reed LaPlant, and a set of Paul McCobb chairs.

Mr. Faherty and his wife, Jill, renovated their 1958 house to make it more family-friendly. "It's going by so fast with our kids," he said of J.P., Greta and Audrey.

In a corner of the living room, a vintage Plycraft chair sits beside a painting by Eric Swenson and a Schoolhouse table and lamp.

dining area framed by the house, you would think this would be a good place for parties, too. But the Fahertys, it seems, rarely entertain.

"As much as we think we'd love to," Mrs. Faherty said, "we really don't."

Mr. Faherty objected: "We do entertain three kids every night, and often their friends."

Even so, the custom white-oak butcher block on the kitchen island is already showing signs of wear. "It's not perfect, and we like it like that," Mr. Faherty said. "We wanted a house that's durable, not fussy."

He added: "Don't look in the garage."

In the master bedroom, a Paul McCobb table and chairs offer a quiet spot to work or read. Ikea cabinets in the bathroom are updated with brass pulls from Schoolhouse. And the kitchen's white-and-wood palette was inspired by the aesthetic of Swedish farmhouses.

COUNTRY, BY A MODERNIST AT PLAY

BY ZOË BLACKLER • PHOTOGRAPHS BY RANDY HARRIS

"I'm not sure it's at all your thing," Alan Orenbuch remembers the real estate broker saying. "It's modern, and pretty strange."

But after a year of negotiations with the owner of a Victorian farmhouse in Millbrook, N.Y., failed to result in a sale, Mr. Orenbuch, an architect, and his partner, Bryan O'Rourke, an interior designer, were ready for something different.

The strange house, which had just come on the market, turned out to be a modernist gem known as the Plastic Tent House, designed in 1974 by the architect John M. Johansen as his own residence.

Mr. Johansen was a member of the Harvard Five, a group of young modernists associated with Harvard's Graduate School of Design in the postwar years. These architects, who included Philip Johnson and Marcel Breuer, built a number of experimental homes that helped reinvent American domestic architecture, many of them in New Canaan, Conn.

The Plastic Tent, one of five so-called Symbolic Houses Mr. Johansen designed between the late 1950s and the 1970s, represented a departure from the modernism practiced by his colleagues. Drawing on the work of the psychoanalyst Carl Jung, he incorporated elements symbolizing the various stages of life — cavelike rooms, bridges, towers, trees — into these houses, taking his work in a new direction.

For his own house, he created a truncated pyramid, 30-foot square in plan. The plastic exterior walls are attached to a lightweight steel frame, from which the second and third floors are suspended; interior stone walls on the first floor provide added support. From inside, the translucent walls glow in the sun, the shadows of falling leaves playing against the surface.

The house is full of Mr. Johansen's signature touches. The bedroom on the first floor is lined with stone, symbolizing the womb. In place of a mirror over the bathroom sink is a window offering a framed view of trees. The second-floor platform overlooking the double-height living area has no protective railings, flirting with danger. And the single room on the third floor — a nestlike wooden box — is suspended from cables so

The Plastic Tent House, near Rhinebeck, N.Y., was designed by John M. Johansen for himself and his wife in 1974. It has semitransparent corrugated plastic walls to create the feeling of a giant tent.

"I'm not sure it's your thing," a real estate broker told Bryan O'Rourke and his partner, Alan Orenbuch, but the men were instantly enchanted by the house.

that it rocks precariously in high winds.

Mr. Johansen lived here for more than 30 years with his wife, Ati, the daughter of the Bauhaus founder, Walter Gropius. But by 2008, they were starting to feel too isolated as an elderly couple, and were finding the upkeep increasingly difficult.

There were several interested buyers, but Mr. Johansen chose Mr. O'Rourke and Mr. Orenbuch because they were designers who knew his work and appreciated the house. The two, who live in a one-bedroom apartment in Manhattan, had been looking for a new weekend retreat for five years. They owned a cottage in the area, but were desperate to find someplace more comfortable, where they could entertain.

They were instantly enchanted by the house. "Within minutes, we knew we wanted it," Mr. O'Rourke said. They bought it in November 2008, on the condition that the Johansens could remain for a year.

The house is now furnished with a collection of midcentury modern furniture that Mr. O'Rourke brought out of storage — mainly bargains he picked up on eBay, like the Eames desk chair he bought for $420 and the knockoff of a well-known George Nelson clock that cost him $70. There are also fortuitous street finds, like the Eames

FROM LEFT: Natural materials like stone contrast with the steel frame covered in corrugated plastic; an imitation Noguchi lamp left by the Johansens hangs in the kitchen; in place of a mirror, a window over a bathroom sink offers a framed view of trees; the translucent walls glow in the sun.

lounge chairs he discovered near their apartment in Greenwich Village. But his most prized pieces are six Robert Guillerme and Hervé and Jacques Chambron dining chairs he bought at a vintage furniture store in Toronto, for $2,000.

Eventually they plan to renovate the kitchen and add a dishwasher, and they would love to rip out the stone bathroom off the living room, which Mr. Johansen said he conceived not as a place for washing up, but for "amorous, contemplative or ceremonial bathing." But they feel a responsibility to be good guardians — to preserve the integrity of the house — particularly since 10 of Mr.

Johansen's 27 houses in the Northeast have been demolished in recent years.

"The space is so dynamic," Mr. O'Rourke said. "John Johansen speaks about the house being alive, and it does feel like that. I hope we get to spend as long here as they did."

As for the Johansens, they have settled happily into life on Cape Cod, where they have a simple two-story cottage. But Mr. Johansen still feels a connection to the house he built, largely with his own hands. "In Jungian thinking, the house is a symbol of its occupant," he said. "I don't own it anymore, but it's still me; I've left something of myself there."

HOW TO RESTORE A MYSTERY HOUSE

BY JULIE LASKY • PHOTOGRAPHS BY ROBERT RAUSCH

Lucia and James Case were living in the affluent Buckhead district of Atlanta and watching their children depart from their square, stolid house when they decided they needed a home that better suited their personalities. "We were never quite comfortable there," Mr. Case, a structural engineer, said of the formal setting.

The house they found in the nearby suburb of Decatur was a different animal. With its sinuous lines, stone facade and low, sloping roof, it looked like a residence for gnomes. Built in 1929, with a 1950s addition, it had been vacant for two years.

And it had a mystery that put the bird-dogging research instincts of Ms. Case into overdrive: All evidence, including the declaration of its former owner, who had lived there for more than 50 years, pointed to the likelihood that it had been designed by the celebrated architect Ernest Flagg. But no records could be found that connected him to the house, or indeed to any house in Georgia.

A Beaux-Arts trained architect, Mr. Flagg (1857 to 1947) designed the Singer Building in New York and the Corcoran Gallery in Washington, among other commissions, before devoting his career to small houses. He was an apostle of efficient design, reviling cellars as hellholes of dampness and attics as reservoirs of junk. His gabled roofs had dormer windows at the ridgelines to draw up air for passive cooling, and his interiors were cleared of any cavities that wasted building material.

All of these features could be found in the gnome home, plus a host of other details so idiosyncratic that the Cases concluded that Mr. Flagg must be the architect. Who else would build on a precise 3-foot-9-inch grid, so that the ceilings were exactly twice that value (7 ½ feet high) at their lowest point? Who else would create 16-inch-thick solid stone and concrete exterior walls, and

The table and chairs in the living room are Indonesian and the sideboard was made in Georgia; all were bought secondhand.

two-inch-thick interior partitions made of jute cord and plaster?

The couple bought the house in 2008, and with Peter Block, an Atlanta architect, and a team of builders and craftsmen, they spent the next three years resolving another conundrum: how to restore it in a way that was true to its presumed architect's principles without compromising their own tastes and comfort.

For all its innovation, the house was poorly suited to the Georgia climate. No air-conditioner had ever been installed. In winter, a subgrade furnace blew hot air through a single giant duct. So part of the $850,000 renovation involved new heating and cooling systems, Mr. Case said. Installing them was made more challenging by the absence of hollow spaces for ductwork, requiring that trenches be dug into the concrete walls.

The Cases also added a 10-foot-deep glass-and-steel extension in back to enlarge the area that currently serves as their living room and expand views onto their 0.6-acre property. They turned the original lengthy living room, with its soaring copper fireplace, into the dining room so they could entertain a large number of guests. The original dining room is now an open kitchen.

Everywhere, the emphasis is on materiality and craft. Walls are hand-plastered. Ceiling beams and kitchen cabinetry are salvaged Georgia pine. And doorknobs, drawer pulls and stair railings are hand-wrought steel. As a result, finishes and details are the substance of the décor, complemented by furnishings collected over the years with an eye to simplicity.

One of several interior designers they consulted advised them to chuck this stuff and start over. "You have a treasure," she told Ms. Case. "You have to be careful what you put in it. I consider your style as Monastic Modern."

But the Cases are done with such decisions. The furniture stays. As Mr. Case said, "We're not as devout as we should be."

Ethereal light is the feature the couple likes best about the front bedroom. The French bed linens came from a resale shop. Andrew Crawford, a sculptor, made the hand-hammered stair railing and much of the house's hardware.

A CASTLE FOR THE KING OF TECHNO

BY JOYCE WADLER • PHOTOGRAPHS BY TREVOR TONDRO

There are a number of things that delight Moby, once the ultimate downtown New York musician, about his castle in the Hollywood Hills: the gatehouse turret, from which the original owner's pet monkey screamed across the canyons when the house was built in 1920s; the lore, both rock 'n' roll and literary and decadent, that has the Rolling Stones living here for a spell, Aldous Huxley residing across the street and porno films shot around the pool; and the hidden room — a former tiki bar — that at one time had a fake grass ceiling and pictures of

Hawaiian dancing girls, which he cannot show you, because this house is so new to him that he can't find the key.

There is also what he calls the "penultimate" Hollywood view, for which you have to go up the stairs to the master bedroom. Be careful: Moby's one rule is no shoes on the rug. O.K., now plop down on the rumpled bed. Looking through the window straight ahead, you can see the canyon fall to the Hollywood Reservoir; to your right and up the hill is the famous Hollywood sign. If he were a Hollywood producer and wanted to impress some actress, Moby says, he'd use that view.

Has he had the opportunity to impress anyone here so far?

"I had a date, which ended up making out under the view of the Hollywood sign, but nothing too crazy," says Moby, who is so slight as to be almost as much of a car-

icature as the drawing on his gray T-shirt. Make that a caricature in pencil. I don't fit in here? No problem. Rub me out. I work alone a lot of the time anyway. In appearance, Moby is either Jules Feiffer's illegitimate son, or he was drawn by him.

But back to the view from the bed and that date. How's that relationship going?

"At present, it's ambiguous. Back in my drinking days, I used to be a little more promiscuous, but now in sobriety, I'm like a nun." A quick correction: "A monk."

It is a heck of an impressive view, he is told; it should have had some effect.

"She came from a very wealthy background," Moby says. (Anyway, what fellow wishes his appeal to be property based?) "Hopefully she was impressed by my wit and character."

Not so long ago, Moby, a musician and

Moby first saw his "crazy shining castle" in the Hollywood Hills, built in the 1920s, from across Beachwood Canyon. The restoration he did included replacing the roof, windows, electricity and plumbing.

composer Billboard once named "The King of Techno," was the hippest of downtown guys, running a teahouse/vegetarian cafe on his Lower East Side home turf, where he sometimes stopped in to wait tables, headlining at the Bowery Ballroom and going on about soy milk (well, he still talks about soy milk).

But now, while he keeps a small apartment in Little Italy, he has moved to Los Angeles, to a castle on three acres with a stone wall, a Disney-esque gatehouse and a kidney-shaped pool. Called Wolf's Lair after its first owner, L. Milton Wolf, a real estate developer, it is a house with old Hollywood flourishes that Norma Desmond would embrace. On the hill overlooking the castle, mounted on a tall pole, is a lamp shaped like a crescent moon, so there will always be the reflection of a moon in the pool, a perfect example of 1920s Hollywood romance. I'll buy you the moon, baby.

For an alternative-music guy, Moby has been doing very well. He has sold 5 million albums and 2 million digital tracks, according to Nielsen SoundScan (his music has been used extensively in soundtracks and commercials). His latest album, "Destroyed," is "broken-down electronic music for empty cities at 2 a.m.," he says, and indeed the music has an echoing, futuristic loneliness.

Moby decided to move to Los Angeles for a number of reasons: New York is so expensive that many of his interesting, creative friends have had to leave; the winters; and that more difficult thing from which to remove oneself, the winter of the soul. The techno musician turns out to have a more debauched past than his persona suggests.

"I stopped drinking a few years ago, and I got to say that the cold and nastiness of New York in February was a lot easier to handle when I was a crazy drunk," he says. "If you're hung over when it's sleeting outside and 40 degrees, it doesn't seem so bad."

Are we talking alcoholism here, A.A. kind of stuff?

"A.A. we're not allowed to talk about, but yeah," Moby says.

What made him stop?

"Simply the consequence of being hung

The house is "the opposite of the houses I lived in growing up, which were very small and dark," Moby said. "Basically, a Freudian in their first three days of school would be able to figure out the psychological impetus, which is creating or moving into the idea that I dreamed of when I was a poor kid."

over 48 hours after being drunk for six hours," he says. "It didn't used to be that way when I was in my 20s. I could stay up till 7 being drunk, and the hangover lasted for two hours. In my 40s, the hangovers lasted for days, and they were debilitating and soul-destroying. I simply had to stop."

If one were to tell a life story through the houses one has lived in, Moby's would be particularly rich. A descendant of Herman Melville whose real name is Richard Melville-Hall, he was born in Harlem, when his father was a graduate student at Columbia.

Moby and his mother moved into her prosperous family's Connecticut home when his father, whom she was divorcing, died driving drunk. His mother, who died of lung cancer, was a sometime secretary and devoted hippie. In 1969, she took him to live in San Francisco.

"My first memory — I don't want to malign my mother, I can almost see her in heaven slapping her head and saying, 'Couldn't you say nice things?' — my first memory is her putting me in this ghetto day care so she could take drugs with her friends," he says, laughing. "My second memory was her and her friends getting really high and sneaking me into X-rated movies."

A few years later Moby and his mother moved back to Connecticut, living sometimes with her parents in their "perfect suburban" center hall colonial house in Darien, and at other times on their own, in grungier, darker places. "We were dirt-poor white trash in arguably the wealthiest white town in the country," Moby says. "I was on food

When Moby first saw the house, the wall above the Gothic fireplace in the living room was covered with shells. He restored the house to its 1920s elegance, preserving details like the wood-beamed ceiling.

stamps until I was 18 and became an adult."

Their homes included a one-bedroom over a garage and a suburban house turned crash pad. "That was basically a mid-'70s drug den," he says, "where her first boyfriend was a Hell's Angel and her second boyfriend was a crazy drug addict who played pedal steel in a country-western bar band."

When his friends' parents came to pick him up for sleepovers at their homes, Moby would give them the address of a nice house.

He became interested in music in high school, when he started going to clubs in New York. At 19, after forming his own band and working as a D.J. at a club, he moved into his own place, in an abandoned factory in Stamford, Conn.

"It had no running water and no bathroom, but there was free electricity, so I could make music, and I was really happy," he says, adding: "I didn't have any romantic life. For some reason, I had a hard time finding a girl who was interested in dating a man who lived in a crack neighborhood with no bathroom and no shower."

In 1986, he moved to Lower Manhattan, where he lived in a series of colorful dumps. There was the tiny two-bedroom on Mott Street owned by a crack addict, and the apartment down the block in a building that had been a Civil War prison.

As the money started rolling in, he started buying extravagant properties. In 2005, he bought four floors of an Upper West Side building but got "really lonely" and sold the apartment a few years later, moving back downtown.

In 2003, he bought a 9,000-square-foot house overlooking the Hudson River in Kent Cliffs, about an hour north of Manhattan. "It wasn't a home," he says. "It was just, I don't know, a weird degenerate country house. I built a disco in it. It was a great place for 30 people to have a drunken week-

The view from the bed in the master bedroom is of the canyon falling to the Hollywood Reservoir; to the right and up the hill is the famous Hollywood sign. **RIGHT:** The guest house was restored by John Lautner in 1961.

end, but it was not such a great place for one person to be there by himself."

He was drinking at this point?

"Oh, boy, yeah, that was the whole reason I had the house," Moby says. "I could go up there for the weekend with friends and just have a whole bunch of lost weekends."

And all these years we thought he was a clean-living vegetarian with an ascetic life.

"The vegetarian part is true, and I work in an ascetic way, but for a good 15 years in New York, I was sort of tragically notorious for always being the last person to leave the bar," he says. "And sometimes inviting everybody in the bar back to my house at 4 in the morning. At one point, I had been at the Mars Bar, and I invited everyone at 4 in the morning back to my house. And at 6 or 7, I had to pee and there were three complete strangers smoking crack in my bathroom. And that is when I realized inviting people back to my house at 4 in the morning was

not such a good idea."

The enormous country house was not such a good idea, either.

"It was huge," Moby says. "It rambled on when I was there by myself. I felt like Orson Welles at the end of 'Citizen Kane.' And this is not a joke, this is not hyperbole — when I renovated the place in Kent, I made the most beautiful bedroom I had ever seen: 1,500 square feet, walls of glass facing north, south, east, 10 beautiful skylights. And I have never had worse insomnia than when I stayed there. So for the last six months that I had that house, I put my mattress in the closet and I slept in the closet. The closet was dark. The problem with the big wall of glass, the sun would come up just as I was trying to go to sleep."

He sold the house. Then, while looking at houses in the Hollywood Hills, he glanced across Beachwood Canyon and saw "this crazy shining castle." The price had dropped 50 percent. He went to see it

and, as he says, fell in love.

The castle needed major work. The roof leaked. The living room walls had been painted a dark gray, the floors had been painted black, the wall above the Gothic fireplace was covered in shells and there was what Moby calls "a low-rent country kitchen from 1979 with strange terra-cotta tiles that were ugly to begin with." He wanted a restoration, not a renovation.

"I basically went through the house and found all the original details from the '20s and tried to renovate the house around all the original architectural elements," he says, which meant getting rid of "everything from 1945 on."

The guest house remodeled by the Frank Lloyd Wright protégé John Lautner in 1961 was exempt from this edict. Moby hired the Los Angeles architecture and design firm of Tim Barber to redo the roof, the kitchen, the plumbing and the wiring, and to replace all the windows and add three bathrooms to the main house. He also plans to turn the tiki barroom into an invitation-only magic theater.

The talk turns to his album, which he wrote while touring, and to the book of photos accompanying it. They're lonely images: deserted cities in the middle of the night, empty tunnels, an office building at 4 a.m. when the cleaning crew has turned on the fluorescent lights.

It's odd that someone who finds beauty in these stark, dehumanized places has chosen to live in what seems like the opposite, a fairy-tale castle, Moby is told.

"It's also, in large part, the opposite of the houses I lived in growing up, which were very small and dark," he says. "Basically, a Freudian in their first three days of school would be able to figure out the psychological impetus, which is creating or moving into the idea that I dreamed of when I was a poor kid."

All he needs now, to go with the castle, is a lady.

The pool house has a view of the Hollywood Hills and the reservoir. OPPOSITE: One of the garages, used as a kickboxing studio: "Hitting and kicking punching bags makes me inexplicably happy," Moby said. An old globe in the corner of the living room is part of a collection.

ACKNOWLEDGMENTS

The New York Times Home section, which debuted on Thursday, March 17, 1977, was one of several weekly features sections introduced as part of an effort by Abe Rosenthal, then executive editor, to attract readers and advertisers to the weekday paper. It survived for 38 years, until the last issue was published on Thursday, March 5, 2015.

Like its siblings — and despite naysaying from some Times traditionalists, especially at first — it was a truly great features section, one that set ambitious journalistic standards for the coverage of subjects previously relegated to the "women's pages" of newspapers. Many editors, reporters and others deserve acknowledgement for making it so strong over the years, among them, Nancy Newhouse, Dona Guimaraes, Jane Traulsen, Stephen Drucker, Penelope Green, Mary Curtis, Barbara Graustark, Michael Cannell and Tom de Kay.

I am personally indebted to a number of extraordinarily talented people I was fortunate enough to work with during my years as editor, including Sara Barrett, Rick Berke, Phaedra Brown, Adam Bryant, Frank Flaherty, Penelope Green, Sam Grobart, Trish Hall, Sandy Keenan, Steven Kurutz, Julie Lasky, Elaine Louie, Farhad Manjoo, Ken McFarlin, Tim McKeough, Anne Raver, Julie Scelfo, Rima Suqi, Bob Tedeschi, Michael Tortorello, Joyce Wadler, Emily Weinstein and so many others. And, of course, Tom de Kay, my immediate predecessor at Home and my longtime collaborator before that, who brought me to the paper and who always makes any project more fun and interesting.

Many thanks also to Charles Miers and Alexandra Tart at Rizzoli for their guidance and enthusiasm about this book; to Phaedra Brown and Ken McFarlin for their hard work on it; and to the editors at the New York Times who made it possible, most especially Alex Ward and Dean Baquet.